Pink Sky at Night

Brightening the Forecast for your Direct Sales Business

Sharon Morgan Tahaney

AuthorHouse™
1663 Liberty Drive
Bloomington, IN 47403
www.authorhouse.com
Phone: 1-800-839-8640

First published by AuthorHouse 5/5/2009

ISBN: 978-1-4389-7863-5 (sc)

Printed in the United States of America
Bloomington, Indiana

This book is printed on acid-free paper.

author HOUSE®

CONTENTS

Pink Sky at Night Strategy

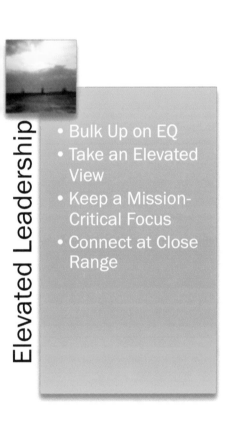

Elevated Leadership

- Bulk Up on EQ
- Take an Elevated View
- Keep a Mission-Critical Focus
- Connect at Close Range

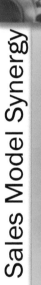

Structural Evolution

- Align with Landscape
- Define Stepping Stones
- Calibrate Sales Leadership
- Keep Your Finger on the Pulse

Sales Model Synergy

- Link What You Have to What They Want
- Align Communications, Learning & Events to Trends & Influencers
- Link Organization to Mission-Critical

PREFACE

Undoubtedly you've heard of blue ocean innovation, blue sky vision, and green-friendly manufacturing. Well, this book brightens the shade and broadens the landscape. It puts a little rose-colored hue in your glasses and a pink sky at night in your forecast.

You'll find here the steps for profitable growth, sustainable growth, quarter after quarter growth, the kind that builds shareholder value. It's not about a temporary blip on the screen. It's about little peaks set on an upward grade. The kind that comes from elevated leadership, bone-deep evolution and sales model synergy.

This book has two intended audiences: the direct selling corporate executive and the direct selling field leader. Typically books are written for one or the other. But here's the start of Pink Sky at Night thinking. It turns a "me" into "we." A partnership with a clear view from both perspectives.

By reading this book, field leaders will see into the thinking behind strategy and tactics laid out by corporate. They will know that to create sustainable growth, you sometimes have to make unpopular decisions. And corporate will get a view from a grounded, street-smart perspective. They will sit in a front row seat in recruiting and know it's everybody's business to get that right.

I've had the great privilege to work in the field and behind the desk. Here's what it taught me. You need both perspectives to see clearly in this business.

A perfect illustration of that fact is an experiment I've conducted with hundreds of leaders dozens of times with the same result.

Here's the experiment: One group of leaders on one side of the room are asked to close their eyes. The other group on the other side are asked to keep their eyes open and look at a picture on the screen. After a minute to process what they see, they're asked to close their eyes while the other group looks at a new picture on the screen. After those two separate viewings, I then place a new picture on the screen. A picture that combines the two previous shots. When I ask both groups to shout out what they see, can you guess what happens every time? The first group see in the new picture only what they had originally seen. The second group see in the new picture only what they had originally seen. Same picture, but due to the influence of a previous experience, they only see what they've seen before.

Perfect proof that the saying is true. We see the world not as it is, but as we are.

A one-sided perspective isn't healthy in direct selling. When corporate leadership and field leadership keep a separate perspective, they begin to live in two different worlds. A "them and us" mentality creeps in and corporate is viewed as an ivory tower and the field as a bit naïve. Neither a true picture.

This book is for both audiences so both see behind the veil of the other. Field leadership sees the why behind strategy and tactics from corporate's perspective, and corporate sees from the feet-on-the-street perspective for a stronger grounding in our business.

Direct selling success depends on this kind of true partnership. We're all working toward the same end and what we do together, after all, really matters.

- We help people become authentic, alive and more than they imagined.
- We create the environment in which children are given the precious gift of example when they see their parents set goals and make them.
- And we provide the means to literally revolutionize a family's living conditions.

That's important work. And it takes a partnership fully engaged, aware and appreciative of one another to make it happen. This book is based on that partnership.

So whether you're a direct selling employee or entrepreneur, every part of this book is relevant. It lets you see what the other half is seeing so you're given twice the perspective and a strong start on creating Pink Sky at Night for your company.

INTRODUCTION

PINK SKY AT NIGHT
Preempts the Warning at Morning

Pink sky at night
Sailors' delight.
Pink sky in morning
Sailors take warning.

When weather had life and death consequences and the methods to forecast it depended on what you could literally see around you, looking to the sky for clues was the "go-to" predictor. We have "go-tos" in our business as well – the kind that create a pink sky forecast for a sunny new day. These "go-tos" are the subject of this book.

But before we dig into them, let's take a closer look at our "pink sky" inspiration. Pink sky at night was a good thing for shepherds and sailors alike. When they looked up and saw a pink sky at night, it meant, no worries for you, shepherds. You can keep your sheep in the fields. And, mariners, rest easy for tomorrow will be a smooth sailing day.

This forecasting method has lived through generations thanks to the life breathed into it with a little poetry. But its origin is in science. So before we bridge the pink sky analogy to our business, let's explore the science. How does a pink sky at night predict sunny skies the next day?

Well, we'll go to a literal discussion and approach the answer like a meteorologist would. When light from the sun meets particles in the atmosphere (such as in clouds), the radiant energy is refracted or scattered. Most of the colors in the spectrum of light are scattered but some are enhanced. The pinkish red light travels longer distances than most, so when clouds are situated in the sky at a longer distance from a setting sun, the pinkish hue is the color that shines through.

So where's the weather forecast in that? Well, first, as you know, weather typically approaches from the West where the sun sets. And as we established, red and pink hues from light travel longer distances than the other colors. Logic tells us that a long-distance cloud from a western setting sun would naturally be situated in the Eastern sky. Since clouds which have already moved to the East mean bad weather in that cloud has already passed those looking up– well, there you have it -- tomorrow is looking good. Some science here…mix in a little poetry…and you've got a memorable forecast.

That long-winded explanation of a literal pink sky at night sets the stage for the point of view of this book. This book is about coloring your business with the kind of action that goes the distance so you brighten your outlook before the night falls.

Panicking, after all, at "pink sky in morning…when direct sellers take warning" is pointless. When your flagship product gets copied by Walmart, too late for an effective solution. When sales force count drops below last year, too late for anything but throwing big promotional dollars at the problem. When your selling proposition becomes predictable and irrelevant, clouds form and customers scatter. When you're losing more leaders than you're gaining, sales force washes away.

Taking Pink Sky action today is a whole lot cheaper, much more effective and creates profitable, sustainable growth. After this book, you can leave the hand-wringing, profit-guzzling, knee-jerk strategy to the folks who relish in re-structuring, work best fighting fires, and are energized by urgencies.

For the rest of us, there's this book and the Pink Sky at Night Strategy.

Pink Sky at Night Strategy will help you start before stagnation. It will map out the structural change, the processes that will take you through implementation and the rocket fuel that will propel you. It is built around bone-deep change, from an above-the-noise perspective, through transformational sales protocol, out-of-the-gate success tactics, buyer psychology, discovery methods and mission critical leadership development.

So pre-empt the warning that comes too late. Think pink sky at night and apply.

- ➢ Pink sky timing
- ➢ Pink sky metrics
- ➢ Pink sky sales team protocol
- ➢ Pink sky recruiting
- ➢ Pink sky new seller success
- ➢ Pink sky communications
- ➢ Pink sky training
- ➢ Pink sky events
- ➢ Pink sky recognition
- ➢ Pink sky leadership

Just like the original shepherd's guide and sailor's tale, combining poetry with science will create your pink sky at night so you sidestep a storm and enjoy a bright new day in your business. Just like "pink sky weather forecasting" direct selling is both an art and a science. It's emotion and math wrapped in the hearts and minds of people.

So read this book and get your head on what counts, your heart on what matters, and your eyes focused on a bright new tomorrow.

In Review:
Pink Sky at Night Strategy

1. This book is about coloring your business with the kind of action that goes the distance so you brighten your outlook before the night falls.
2. Direct selling is an art and a science, emotion and math wrapped up in the hearts and minds of people.
3. Pink Sky at Night Strategy is built on elevated leadership, bone-deep evolution and sales model synergy.
4. Pink Sky Thinking is around structural change, buyer psychology, the discovery process, and leadership growth.

CHAPTER ONE

PINK SKY AT NIGHT TIMING
Starts Before Stagnation

No doubt, you've heard the old saying that involves putting "lipstick on a pig." When you're relying solely on carrots to entice action or you dress up a weak comp plan or stale selling proposition with promotional bling, well, it's the perfect setup for this saying to come to mind.

Promotions promising trips and diamonds and kitchen appliances stir up excitement and provide a spike in sales. That's good, of course. But with the upside comes a downside. There is the danger that the spike distracts you from the long game. Your focus gets fixed on the moment and foggy about the future. You get lulled by the euphoria of beating the week and blind sighted by what's coming next year. Now obscures next. And next could be that emerging trend that takes you out of business, or a passive sales force that's waiting for the next widget of the week to get moving.

When profits count and shareholder value is at stake, not knowing what's around the corner and creating passivity from your sales force just aren't good actions for meeting forecast. In other words, the "lipstick on a pig" approach is not the road to sustainable, profitable growth…the kind that creates quarter after quarter of sales and profit improvement.

That comes with pink sky thinking or a deeper kind of change. Structural change. The kind of change that comes before irrelevance, before entitlement, before passivity and before stagnation.

So why don't companies change with the times more readily, more easily, more successfully? Why aren't all leaders "pink sky at night" thinkers?

Well, real change -- bend-in-the-road kind of change -- is uncomfortable. No, it's more than that. It's gut wrenching. Tough to tackle. Staying steady, on the other hand, sticking with the tried and true, the "proven" methods, on-path and in between the lines feels safe which makes settling in to sameness feel right. Then it happens. You get used to just getting by. You go numb and less responsive to the declining trend line. Less flexible to new ideas. More committed to defending the status quo. Stuck, static and stale.

You sacrifice tomorrow for the "safety" of today. Worn out ways have created ruts so deep, the entire company rides along without blinking.

Time for Pink Sky at Night leaders. The kind who shake themselves out of settling for sameness. The kind who become nimble instead of numb…who bend the culture so they protect the company. How do you become nimble? Light on your feet? Making news and building roads?

First, it helps to fortify your gut. Taking a lesson from the work of Jim Collins is a good start in bulking up on the strength it takes to forge real change needed to produce Pink Sky at Night.

Jim Collins wrote an article about the commonalities among the 70 companies still in existence from the original Fortune 500. Those 70 companies had three significant things in common. One, they built a portfolio of flywheels upon which to grow. Two, they were run by cost-obsessed executives. And three, they practiced "creative destruction" within their own walls. The other 430 companies that had fallen from the Fortune 500 had allowed the cool start-ups to eclipse them in the "creative" arena. Creative destruction from outside their walls resulted in actual destruction **of** their walls.

Rather than letting the new kid competitor come up with the game-changing idea, make it your mission to uncover it yourself. Even when the game-changing idea makes your flagship product obsolete. If you don't do it, history has shown that someone else will. So build up your tolerance for change and destroy the old by replacing it with the new before your competition does it for you.

At this point, hopefully, you've embraced the idea that prepping for tomorrow with Pink Sky at Night Thinking is critical. You realize it involves more than applying a promotional layer of paint, that it digs deep into the structure and culture of your business, and it is an exercise for now, not later. So at this point, let's start turning the why into what and how. First, we'll dig beneath the surface to discover the "what" in Pink Sky at Night Strategy.

1. It starts before stagnation.

2. It happens so "promotional layering" doesn't.

3. It doesn't let "now" obscure "next."

4. It doesn't settle for sameness.

5. It avoids the ruts of worn out ways.

6. It is nimble, not numb.

7. It bends the culture to protect the company.

8. It practices "creative destruction" within it own walls.

CHAPTER TWO

PINK SKY AT NIGHT THINKING
Explores Beneath the Surface from an Above-The-Noise Perspective

When my youngest son, Mitchell, was little, he collected rocks. On every walk, he would come home with a pocket full of pebbles in every shape, weight and size. One day Mitchell and I were walking together on a little country road when he stopped, reached down and picked up a rock. As he looked up and handed it to me he said simply, "This one's for you." It was the rock you see here. I've had it with me for fifteen years. It reminds me of why I love what we do. Over the years the sand, rain and the knocking together of other rocks had chipped away the exterior to reveal the magic inside, a heart as beautiful as one chiseled by an artist.

Seem familiar? We don't create the masterpiece inside people we touch in this business, we simply release it. That's the payback. The power. Our purpose. We create the environment for people to discover who they are and what they want so the strength they carry inside can be revealed to themselves and everyone else.

That's a heavy mission we share. And to manage that kind of lifting, it makes sense that we position ourselves on higher ground. To rise above the fray and take an elevated view so we see the depth of what's possible.

As leaders in direct selling, we carry the vision, so we must keep that elevated perspective. We also carry the path. The path requires a different perspective, a close range perspective. Close enough to scrape away distractions and focus on the essence of what's beneath the surface...the actions and tactics that will take us to greatness.

Pink Sky at Night Thinking combines this kind of elevated vision and tactical sculpting. This long-view/close range dichotomy is the dance of transformation. It's fluid and open, yet disciplined and deliberate. How can these contradictions co-exist? Remember, our business is a contradiction. It is both an art and a science. It's forecasted with formulas yet driven with emotion.

So let's approach the contradiction one position at a time. First, the long view. The one that allows you to see the big picture and carry the vision.

Define Mission Critical.
Create an Opportunity Focused Culture to Attract and Mobilize Sellers

It starts by clarifying what's mission critical for your business. I have found that when you rely on volunteers to market your product as we do, mission critical to long-term success is the ability to attract and mobilize new sellers. In other words, having an opportunity-focused culture is mission critical to most growing direct sellers.

Does that mean you become recruiting myopic? All things are secondary to the business opportunity?

Product managers will be relieved to know the answer is no. No, very simply because everything works together to create the business opportunity. The attraction of a new seller starts with the exclusivity and value of your product. If your product is found on retail shelves around every corner, or if the price tag is outside the price corridor of your market, or the value is unclear and your selling proposition is distasteful, boring or time-guzzling, you will not attract new sellers. Attracting sellers means first attracting consumers. Consumers who value your product and enjoy the buying experience will be open to the thought of building a business around it. This is where an opportunity-focused culture begins. With your product.

Sellers must believe in your product to be passionate about sharing it. That's when they will feel authentic; they will be sincere; they will make money. And you? You will grow revenue with every new seller you attract.

So being "opportunity-focused" starts with building value in your product, keeping it exclusive to your sellers, pricing it in reach of the market and creating a desirable and easily duplicated experience for selling it.

The upcoming chart will keep the focus in full view. You'll see here that your business opportunity must be the face to the world. The public can readily see the opportunity on your Web site, in your catalogs and flyers and at all your events.

The return on time for recruiting must be rich and rewarding. Examine where you focus your recognition. Put building a team first on the list and most powerful in your emphasis. And see that you've made it clear there's real value in building a team from an earnings perspective.

Look at your career path, programs, recognition, training and earnings plan to be sure there is a strong "pull to the top." When one team level is reached, you have a roadmap, incentive plan and learning experience that immediately focuses your sales force on the next step upward in team size and in title.

Keep a keen eye on the entry experience into your business. Be certain it's inviting, easy, and the return on investment is clear.

And lastly, link every department into this opportunity focus. Have each one examine their areas with a critical eye on process and contact with the field. Are they complicating the business in any way? Are they skipping over the business opportunity to focus solely on product? Is their contact with the field consistent, courteous, and field-savvy? Do they have tactics and discussions around how their areas could exalt and enhance the business opportunity?

Building an opportunity-focused culture involves everyone from all angles at all times. It means creating new measures, drivers and income-enablers in your compensation plan. It means having systems readily available for everyone to plug into. All of these are unveiled in a Pink Sky at Night strategy and are, therefore, in this book. For now, we'll stay at 30,000 feet and look at the second Mission Critical focus for profitable growth in direct selling.

Pink Sky at Night Strategy
Building an Opportunity-Focused Culture

Three "Musts" for a Recruiting Culture

1. Product has mass appeal and in value and price corridor of mass market.

3. Selling method is simple. See one…do one.

5. Recruiting is supported with tools integrated throughout selling system & rewarded with recognition and return.

Face to the world screams this focus:

- Your Web site
- Your Catalogs and flyers
- Your community events

Return on time to Recruit must be rich	"Pull" must be consistent and powerful	Entry into business must be easy
• Saturate message •Best Recognition •Highest awards for Recruiting	• PR Reprints • Growth Programs •recruiting focused hotlines & events • Stable kit strategy	• 24/7 recruit registration • Easy online registration • Convenient payment options • First steps clear

Every Department & Action must Exalt Recruiting & Recruiters

- Recruiting campaigns are the key promotional campaigns for the year
- Events spotlight builders and act as platforms to launch recruiting campaigns
- Consistency with key messages
    - Step up the career path
    - Step into Leadership
    - Building Team Size is ticket to consistent income
    - Consistent personal recruiting maximizes your influence for team recruiting and your ability to build team size and find new leaders.

We all know that fire burns hottest at the source. What's the source of passion and commitment in our business? I have found it to be with an aspiring leader. Whether that means a future leader in a leadership qualification program or an established leader in a growth program, the source of real heat is squarely in the middle of that pocket of passion.

This is the "portfolio of flywheels" phenomenon Jim Collins identified as a key to sustainable growth. Creating these pockets of passion throughout your organization is mission critical to a "Pink Sky at Night" prediction for profitable growth. The reason? These pockets, these leaders, are the direct link to the ultimate performance indicator in our business – active sales force count. A leader creates the energy for an entire team to focus on growth. Recruiting becomes a mission. It's more than a paycheck. It's the fulfillment of purpose. This kind of passion, motivation and leadership grows from relationships and close-range guidance. The more real leaders you create in your business, the greater your success at building sales force count.

So, a two-prong focus will ultimately take you to the top-line sales number that is sitting right now in front of you on your goal chart. I know you have one. That sales number is the lagging indicator. The path to achieving it is through recruiting, activation, and retention of your sales force. That path is created by having an opportunity-focused culture and a company-wide commitment to building strong leaders.

Define Mission Critical

Build "portfolio of flywheels" by building leadership ranks

Make Teams the focus for leadership development, recruiting and sales management

- Empower and expect leadership from Field Leaders
- Glorify the act of promoting Leaders

Look and act like an "Opportunity-focused" company
- Have simple, duplicable selling method & messaging
- Have product with mass appeal and hits consumers value
- Use Active Sales Force Count as primary predictor
- Make the "star" of ALL Events recruiting and leadership development
- Design key promotions around recruiting and leadership development.
- Integrate the act of recruiting in all customer interactions
- Provide numerous methods of recruiting support.

While we're addressing the topic of an "above the noise" perspective, let's take an elevated view of a successful direct selling company. What is the framework? Here are the pillars upon which to build:

1. Product: Have a product with a distinctive over the competition, exclusivity to your sellers, and within the price corridor of your market.
2. Selling Method: Offer your product through a selling method that's simple to duplicate and adds value beyond buying for your customers.
3. Sales Force: Attract and mobilize a sales force with an opportunity-culture and a leadership development focus.
4. Financial Responsibility: Manage your finances to your targeted ROS with a keen eye on inventory, distribution, margin, and operating expenses.

5. Management Team: Have the management team who can do the four above.

Pink Sky at Night Transformation

If your leadership structure, your compensation plan, your programs, events, and learning curriculum aren't aligned with your mission critical focus, then it may be time you make some of those bone-deep structural changes that will take your business forward.

Having led transformation efforts in a variety of situations and companies, I've included "go-bys" to guide your thinking.

The transformation process can feel like bowling on the beach. It can get bogged down and feel painfully slow. To help smooth out and speed up the process, here are the lessons I've learned from real world change management. Some we've covered here and some need only be listed for you to grab them and go.

Lessons Learned in Structural Transformation

1. Create your "Mission Critical" landscape. Know the destination before you create the stepping stones.

2. Build the change team who will guide the transformation with a mix of expertise. Diverse and opinionated people make for great debate and a rounded out plan.

3. Before you implement anything, connect with your key influencers in the field for buy-in. Tell them "why" before you share "what."

4. Map out "nirvana" (your perfect plan) and then build a bridge to get you there. The transition plan to the change is as critical as the plan itself. Provide a promotional bridge that awards the behaviors defined in the longer-term change before you institute the change. Reward the behavior before it becomes the rule.

5. Define new measures and corresponding drivers, systems, and support. What are the key performance indicators to build your new foundation for growth?

6. Communicate often and from every angle. Internally and with the field.

7. Link all departments and disciplines to the new vision and new path.

8. Celebrate small successes to fortify courage because it will get a little dark en route to a new day. Every measurement you've defined as critical deserves recognition.

9. Stay close to your financials. Know margin target, inventory goal, distribution pressures, and operating expenditures. Make a profit and watch everyone climb on board with the change.

10. Assign clarity around structural changes with a "From-To" guide. A From-To template follows with suggestions of the structural change you will want to clarify.

11. Be sure to provide this same clarity for the sales model. A From-To guide outlining the change necessary in the sales model to align with a structural change in your business will link all departments with the new measures, drivers and methods to make sure your sales model morphs right along with your structural change. A template follows to get you started.

12. Find strength in the fact you're protecting the company, not necessarily the culture. You're creating the culture. Stay true, focused and confident.

Structural Change: From…To

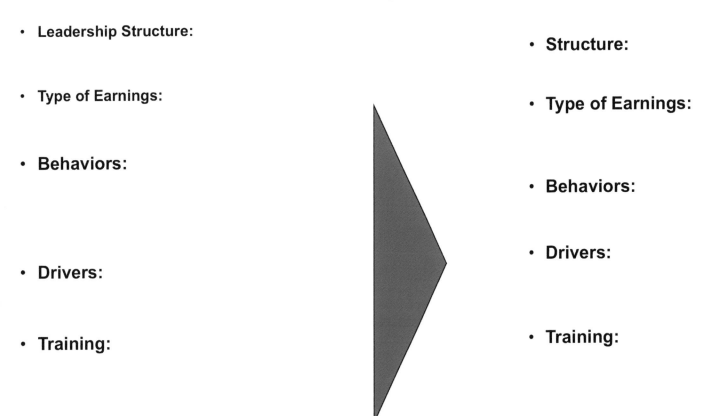

- Leadership Structure:

- Type of Earnings:

- Behaviors:

- Drivers:

- Training:

- Structure:

- Type of Earnings:

- Behaviors:

- Drivers:

- Training:

Sales Model From…To

- Events

- Promotions

- Programs

- Communications

- Events

- Promotions

- Programs

- Communications

Sculpt the Tactics

Now, let's start digging beneath the surface to sculpt the tactics that will release the magic inside our Mission Critical Focus.

First, before decisions are made on metrics and tactics, ask yourself some key questions about your proposed plan.

- What behavior do I want to drive?
- How do I measure it?
- What is it now?
- What do I want it to be?
- What is the value of the difference?

Examine your Compensation Plan

Your compensation plan is a key driver toward behavior modification and results. Is recruiting a key enabler of income generation in your plan? Is your leadership level clearly defined in your plan and behaviors clearly differentiated from aspiring leaders and sellers? Your sales force will go where the money is. What percentage of payout do you devote to sales? To team leadership? Are you balanced? Are you competitive landing somewhere between 35% and 50% of retail paid to your sales force?

There are a plethora of books on compensation plans outlining plan options, emphasis and structures. The point here is to make your compensation plan a key tool in your mission critical focus and to make the analysis of your compensation plan a continual part of your Pink Sky planning. Measure and evolve it to be sure you're getting a return in leadership growth and seller count. Is the leadership level clearly identified and qualifications to get there strong enough and over a long enough time to create real leaders who will step into the role with passion and commitment? Remember, the leader's strength is your most dependable path to building sales force count.

Create Stepping Stones

You know your ultimate destination. You know the sales number you want to achieve. Now it's time to create the stepping stones that will get you there.

Since sales is a lagging indicator and comes as a result of performance in such areas as recruiting, activation of new recruits, the health of your leadership pipeline, seller retention, and leadership growth, a smart approach is to identify metrics in these areas that serve as your "stepping stones" on your path toward sales. Shouting out your sales target and saying, "Let's go get this!" won't give you power to get there.

Your path is more sure when it's built on foundational "stones" that step by step take you to your goal. As the saying goes, "Build it and they will come." Drive these metrics and sales will come.

Five Stones To Build Your Path

1. Recruits per sales force member.
2. Percent of new sellers who sell within their first 30 days.
3. Percent of new sellers still selling at 120 days.
4. Percent of sellers in your leadership pipeline.
5. Percent of leaders in a growth program.

Or possibly your five stones look like this:

1. Number of new sellers added by mid-year and end of year.
2. Percent of customers attending your selling venue who are new.
3. Number of clients/shows per seller per period.
4. Percent of clients/customers you retain from one season to the next.
5. Number of leaders you build each quarter.

Here's the point. Target and communicate the actions that will make the biggest difference in getting you to your sales result. Lay down your stepping stones for all to see. You carry the path so be specific, be clear and be generous in sharing it with everyone.

Create a Map for Implementation

Your role as a leader is to show the path and direct all parties in how to walk it together. Implementation is critical. I have always found clarity of communication begins with an overview, a guide that provides a snapshot of the whole picture in one view.

I've included a template here that may help you organize your thoughts for implementation. Set up your guide in a similar way in which you define your new metrics or stepping stones, the drivers for each, the communication highlights, the reminder to link to all departments, and the focus you'll need to duplicate your efforts and enjoy growth. It's a great implementation guide once you've established your mission critical focus and your foundational "stones" for sales growth.

Sample Pink Sky at Night Implementation

Measure

Create New Measures for New Focus

Path
- ___recruits per seller
- ____% qualification rate
- ___% of seller count in Leadership Pipeline
- _____% of Leader count in Leader Qualification Program
- _____% selling after 120 days
- Enrolled sellers X seller % X Productivity$ = Sales

Drivers
- Defined and specific success habits.
- Team Recruiting Goal
- Team Size Goal
- 1-on-1 coaching identifying ___% in leadership pipeline

Leader Qualification program
Leader Growth Program
New Seller Fast Star program

Communicate

Create Simple and Duplicatable Business
- Easy entry
- Every Step training
- "I Can Do That" selling process
- Systems to plug in to

Breathe Life into Our Opportunity
- Elevate the message above money
- Show Return on recruiting is worth investment of time
- Use New Leader Training as platform
- Use workshops to reinforce key messages
- Maintain Consistent and powerful "pull"

Grow

Pink Sky
Grow Seller Count
Focus

Link Sales Team Incentives
- Recruits (normalized)
- Leadership Pipeline growth
- Sales qualifier linked to Plan

Link & Integrate all Departmental Functions
- Promotions   Events
- Communications   Training
- Sales Support   Customer Care
- Finance
- Internal Reports
- Manufacturing
- Distribution

Connect

Establish Your Leadership Guide

While we're talking about guides to keep you on path, you will need to establish a Leadership Guide that clearly connects the number of aspiring leaders, added leaders, and retained leaders to your sales goal. Based on your history or knowledge of average team size for leaders, what will it take in leadership numbers to get to your ultimate sales number? How many in your leadership pipeline do you need? (Leadership pipeline refers to those sales force members who are positioned just prior to your first leadership level.) How many do you need entering your leadership qualification program? How many new leaders do you need to create each quarter? How many do you expect to lose? And what are the actions to impact each of these leadership concerns?

The sample here may jumpstart your thinking in each of these critical areas of leadership development:

Build your Portfolio of Leaders

Turn your sales goal into leadership #s: _____ added into Leadership Pool   _____ ending count of aspiring leaders
_____added new leaders   _____ ending count

What do we need? HOW do we do it?

Improve # of aspiring leaders
- Reinforce consistent recruiting
- Create Leader Development Training Tool
- Reinforce with targeted promotional campaigns
- Create "New Seller Roadmap" that takes them to leadership
- Use events as platforms to recognize new leaders

Improve entries into Leadership Qualification
- Brand your Leadership Lifestyle
- Create Presentation of Leadership Lifestyle to attract aspiring leaders
- Make aspiring leaders the stars of your events
- Reinforce consistent Recruiting

Increase Success Rate of Leadership Qualification
- Provide Mentoring Training module for aspiring leaders
- Provide Focused breakouts at events for aspiring leaders

Improve Leader Retention
- Counter vulnerability of weak months
- Increase leader count in Growth Programs.
- Reinforce Consistent Recruiting
- Expect all leaders to attend your New Leader Training
- Sales Leaders conduct Action Planning with field leaders
- Recognize Leaders for Team Size growth

To keep the process moving, I've found it helpful to keep the day to day actions you'll need to perform to manage your progress toward your goal. Here is a sample view you may find helpful to build your own guide for daily maintenance.

Managing the *Pink Sky* Model

Analysis
Recruits/sales per SF
Recruits/sales per team
New Seller Activation
New Seller Retention
Leadership Pool
Leader Count
Leader Retention

Leader Retention
% in Growth Program
Event Training Focus
On-line support

Commission Payout
Sales %
Sales Management %

Leader Growth
New Leader Training
Advanced Leadership
Field mtgs
Regional Coaching
Growth Program

Sustain Growth

Leader Development
Mentoring Tool
Qualification Program
Event Focus

1st Level Leader Development
New Seller Advancement
Tool Driving level

Add a Little ESP to Achieve Your Sales Number

Direct selling, as you know, is mathematically predictable. In every direct selling company, you have key performance indicators that come together to create your sales results. This is basic knowledge and will give you a better sense of control over your results when you bring the top three to the top of your thinking and planning. The top three I call ESP simply because of the clarity they give you in predicting your future sales results.

E stands for Enrolled Sellers, your real sales force members who are inside your "active" standards.

S stands for Sellers who have sold something that month. For this metric, you calculate the percentage of Enrolled Sellers who actually sold something in the month.

P stands for Productivity, the average dollar amount these sellers sold that month.

Using ESP in your business will allow you to see fluctuations and diagnose issues. When you see Seller percentage take a dive or a spike or productivity trending unusually high or low, you can then compare corresponding merchandising and promotional efforts and know which ones worked and which ones didn't. If Seller percentage and Productivity are trending without big dives or blips, then it becomes crystal clear where your laser like focus should be – on building that first indicator, Enrolled Seller count.

ESP is also a great way to better understand where you stand in reaching a goal. Take your ultimate monthly sales goal and back into the Enrolled seller count you'll need to make that goal. To do that, divide your monthly sales goal by the Productivity number you're trending, then divide that number by your trend in percent of sellers selling, the end result will be the number of Enrolled sellers you need to meet your monthly sales goal.

Whether you're using ESP to diagnose issues or to calculate the number of Sales Force you need to meet a sales goal, this basic little direct selling formula will give you insight and guidance.

Pink Sky at Night Thinking

1. Direct Selling is based on formulas yet driven by emotion.

2. It requires both elevated vision and tactical sculpting.

3. Focusing on an opportunity culture and leadership development have proven to be two mission critical areas for sustainable, profitable growth.

4. Being "opportunity-focused" starts with building value in your product, keeping it exclusive to your sellers, pricing it in reach of your market, and creating a selling experience that's desirable and easily duplicated.

5. The fire of growth burns hottest in the center of a pocket of passion – the source of which is an aspiring leader.

6. Your sales force will go where the money is. Is team-building a key enabler of income generation in your compensation plan?

7. Establish the metrics that will produce the end product of sales. Starting with your sales target and saying, "Let's go get this!" isn't a path to making that dictate come true. The path is built on foundational "stones" that will take you forward one step at a time.

8. Use guides to provide clarity and focus while keeping action steps in front of your entire team.

9. Keep an ESP trendline on Enrolled sellers, % Selling, and Productivity. Giving yourself ESP in your business will help you better diagnose issues and establish the sales force count you'll need to meet a monthly sales goal.

10. Walk through transformation guided by the lessons learned in real world application.

11. Be loyal to the company, not necessarily to the culture. Create the culture that will protect the company.

CHAPTER THREE:

PINK SKY AT NIGHT SALES LEADERSHIP
Transforms roles & behaviors

There was a study by psychologist Henry Goddard about the importance of the words we use and their impact on people. Mr. Goddard hooked folks up to an "ergograph" to measure responses. One group was given encouraging words, positive words, empowering words. With that group a surge of energy registered on the ergograph. Another group was given discouraging words, negative criticism, and a dismal outlook. You can probably guess what happened. Energy took a nosedive.

Now I start this chapter on Sales Leadership with this little study in human motivation because this is the stuff solid sales leadership is made of. In our business, those in the front row working at close range with a sales force have to be more than a wiz with a computer spread sheet. Sales leaders today have to be focused on both relationships and results. They spend a great deal of time on what can't be measured or graphed. And it's been proven over and over again in our business that how people feel has everything to do with how they perform. A volunteer sales force wakes up every day and based on how they feel, will either jump up and map out their plans to drive their business…or roll over and hit the snooze button. Sales leaders make the difference in their choices.

Your goal as a sales leader is to continue to move your sales force toward the right in the Emotional Continuum. Where is your sales force right now? Where are you?

Emotional Continuum

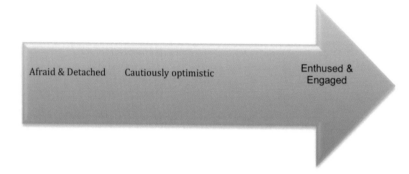

Continue movement to "enthused and engaged" with these actions:
- Put purpose behind goals
- Shore up knowledge & build confidence
- Share Success Stories
- Communicate often and from all angles
- Exalt Organizations With Promoted Leaders
- Signal respect for Top Field Leadership

Intangible Assets Translate into Economic Value

Some may think talking about emotions and feelings is a soft-headed exercise and has no place in business. The fact is, in our business, emotions are more than feelings. They're energies. And recognizing this fact along with respecting the spirit of human motivation is what great organizations are all about.

Sales leaders are in the front row seat and work at close range to influence and inspire a sales force. So it's the company's job to be sure their role is defined as such and their job is supported with resources so they have time to focus on awakening the spirit and guiding actions toward goals.

This doesn't mean the job of a sales leader is an unstructured happy hour. It does mean the job of a sales leader is connected to the strategically vital. And that means it's connected to your mission critical emphasis of building your sales force count by building your field leadership.

Not every sales team has this focus. Some are still operating like glorified customer care representatives fielding ordering questions, scouting information, debating exception policies. None of that feeds the spirit or energizes commitment. It just wastes time.

Sales team operating protocol, on the other hand, is clear, supported with resources and linked to mission critical.

I've seen sales teams who are quite efficient at managing all the things of their job. In fact, they do quite well with management tasks. But the problem is this. A sales team leads people. You manage things but you lead people. And being the most efficient manager in the world won't make you an effective sales leader. Being an effective sales leader is so much more than doing things right. It means doing the right things--the things that build people and release greatness.

It's easy to see the difference in a sales team that manages and one that leads when you look at how each spends its time. A sales team that tries to be all things to all people and spends the bulk of its time informing and explaining, clarifying promotions, scouting information, refereeing exceptions and performing administrative tasks will not have the time to focus on your mission critical emphasis on leadership development. They may be efficient, but not that effective at moving your company toward profitable growth.

If, however, you support your sales team so they can focus their time on the strategically vital – on attracting new sellers, activating new sellers, identifying future leaders, mentoring future leaders through qualification, and coaching new leaders, then you'll have a team that's bringing you the biggest return on your investment.

So here's the main point -- if your sales team is spending an inordinate amount of time on functional efficiencies, on issuing goals without roadmaps, pleading action toward goals without coaching, screaming about goals without customized action plans to get each leader there, your team is not as effective as it could be. So let's talk how a sales team carries the vision, belief and the path to inspire trust, commitment, and performance.

You build trust from your sales force by being trustworthy. To have an agreed-upon guide to govern decisions and actions is a great place to start in creating the landscape to inspire trust.

Here is a sample set of guidelines that may be a starting place for you and your sales team. Read these and work with your sales team to develop your own set of guiding principles. Then keep them prominent and use them as your true-north in making decisions.

Guiding Principles

Make the business simple, profitable & fun.
Earn trust.
Lead with passion.
Build and protect relationships.
Remember our first customer is the sales force.
Keep every promise.
Implement flawlessly.
Value differences.
Ensure sustainability.

So the role of a sales leader starts with more than competence. It requires character as well. Here is an overview of the role of a sales leader in a regional position:

Role of Regional Sales Leader

- Measures all decisions against principles.
- Balances field influence with company responsibilities.
- Calculates the impact (hard & soft) of every proposal brought forward.
- Builds relationships through influence, not position.
- Knows and does the things that give the highest return.
  - Grows active sales force count
  - Develops leaders
- Provides field training.
  - Communicates the vision and strategy of the company

- o Attracts new sellers and new leaders through workshops (online, live, by phone)
- Is accountable for results beginning with weekly results. Expresses goal in terms of sales force count needed to reach goals.
- Builds trust and belief.

Contact, Contact, Contact

The big picture for a regional sales leader is clear. Now what about the specifics? What are the actions that prove to bring results? The answer is in three words: contact, contact, contact. Whether the contact is face to face, in an online Webinar, over the phone or by email or letter, contact that's consistent, customized and focused is the most effective tool of a sales leader.

Personalized Coaching to Top 20%

I have found one of the most powerful contact tools for return on time is the personalized coaching call or visit conducted with your top 20% of field leadership. We all know the 80/20 principle holds true in our business. Around 80% of your results typically come from the top 20% of your leadership. So this is your focus to get the best return on your time. Establish a 30 minute call time or visit consistently on your calendars. Center the call around these areas:

- the leader's personal business.
- who's next on her team to step into leadership.
- the team's status in sales force count, seller percentage (percent of team selling that week or month), productivity (the average dollar amount the sellers sold that week/month), and the resulting total sales figure. Take a look at the trendline in all four indicators for the team to spot areas to celebrate and those needing corrective action.
- Discuss ideas to counter falling trend in seller activity and/or productivity. Activity drivers for the leader to use may be corporate-supplied sales force promotions that drive involvement and new contact methods between the leader and her team. Do the same with productivity. Discuss how to leverage current corporate supplied merchandising offers that drive add-on sales.
- Based on the leader's specific goal, use ESP to calculate the size team needed to reach that goal.
- Brainstorm ways to add new recruits to the team.

- Discuss who on the team are candidates to move up to leadership.
- Email the field leader the action plan agreed upon at end of the call.
- Send a personalized note complimenting the seller identified as a candidate for leadership. Point her to the next steps to grow.

Weekly Conference Call or Webinar

The next tactic for a regional sales leader is a consistent targeted and focused conference call or webinar. This is a great time to recognize the behaviors that align with the "stones to build your future." Appoint a featured speaker each week who can speak to what's worked. Keep the call focused and on time.

Live Field Meetings

The best contact will always be the face to face kind. Schedule visits in the field as often as your budget will allow contributing to sales meetings, celebrations and Business Opportunity events. Be sure you take full advantage of the trip by issuing a challenge for recognition before you arrive and a challenge for recognition as you leave. A reception with you prior to the meeting or dessert with you afterwards are great ways to award achievers.

Field Learning

A proven way to turn an "afraid and detached" sales force into an "enthused and engaged" one is to shore up knowledge and build relationships. A regional sales leader is in the perfect position to build confidence by taking a consistent and planned approach to the education and development of your sales force. Workshops focused on the benefits of leadership, the steps to become leaders, the recruiting process, activation of new sellers – these are all learning modules ideal for a sales leader to facilitate. Today's sales leader should not be remembered as an overly caffeinated cheerleader, but as a coach, mentor and inspiration.

A Regional Sales Leader Contact Plan

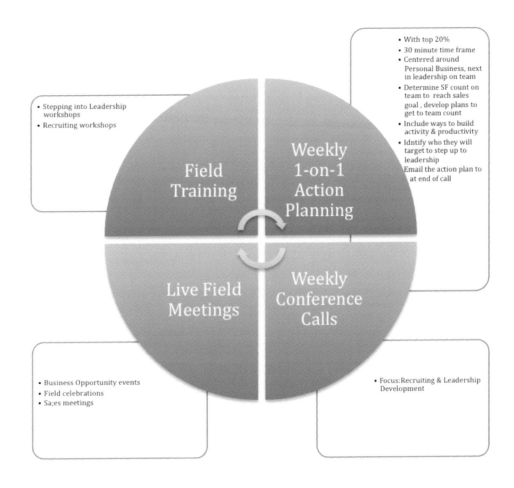

- Stepping into Leadership workshops
- Recruiting workshops

- With top 20%
- 30 minute time frame
- Centered around Personal Business, next in leadership on team
- Determine SF count on team to reach sales goal , develop plans to get to team count
- Include ways to build activity & productivity
- Idntify who they will target to step up to leadership
  Email the action plan to at end of call

Field Training

Weekly 1-on-1 Action Planning

Live Field Meetings

Weekly Conference Calls

- Business Opportunity events
- Field celebrations
- Sa;es meetings

- Focus:Recruiting & Leadership Development

Weekly one-on-one Coaching Call Between Company and Regional Sales Leader

Corporate has a responsibility in the contact business as well. Contact between the company and the regional sales leadership team is also a weekly, focused and planned event.

- Review Regional's goal and progress toward goal.
- Keep a log of those identified by the Regional as future leaders and those in the leadership qualification program.
- Set specific goal for next week for recruiting and for sales. Discuss current drivers and percent of leaders participating in "growth programs."

Call Agenda
- Greatest accomplishment since last call?
- What you wanted to get done but didn't?
- Challenges you're facing right now?
- Opportunities available to you next week?
- Those you're moving into leadership?
- Those you're mentoring through leadership qualification?
- Your progress toward your goal?
- What you're committed to do before our next call?
- How you will drive recruiting, activity, productivity to meet next week's goal?

Keeping a Sales Team Progress Report

Asking your Regional sales team to chart their progress toward goals on a weekly basis is a great way to be sure your focus stays on the strategically vital. The Regional weekly "progress report" would chart:

Recruits
- Your week's forecast against the weekly actual
- Each week's percent to monthly goal

Leadership Pipeline (level prior to leadership level)
- Monthly goal
- Actual Additions
- Monthly Actual

Enrolled Sellers (active sales force)
- Monthly total

- Sellers selling that week/month
- Monthly percent selling (activity)

Aspiring Leaders in Qualification
- Monthly Goal
- Monthly Actual

Sales
- Monthly Goal
- Weekly forecast
- Weekly Actual
- Percent each week to monthly goal

Then on this progress report each sales leader answers the following:

What happened this week?
- Recruiting
- Leadership Pipeline
- Enrolled Seller Count
- Leaders in qualification

Your Immediate Actions?
- Recruiting
- Activation of new recruits
- Leadership Pipeline
- Leadership in Qualification

Your Needs from Corporate?
- Recruiting
- Leadership Pipeline
- Seller activity
- Productivity
- Pull to leadership
- Sales

Having your Regional sales leaders keep this kind of analysis on a weekly basis of their business will prepare them for your coaching call and weekly group call.

Mentoring Process

Mentoring people forward is an integral part of any sales leader's job. The guide below may prove helpful to you in building your mentoring system.

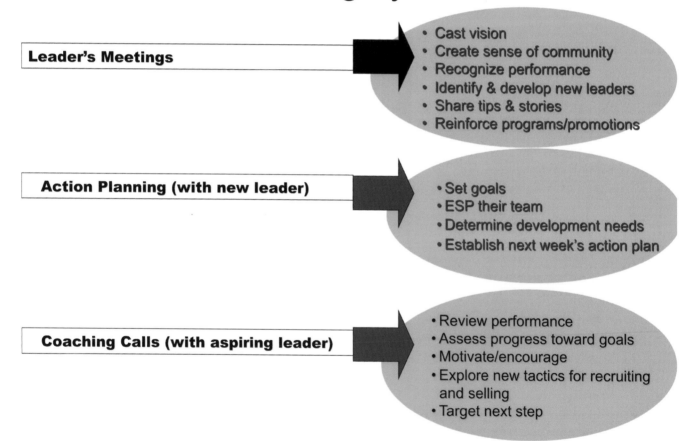

Mentoring System

Leader's Meetings
- Cast vision
- Create sense of community
- Recognize performance
- Identify & develop new leaders
- Share tips & stories
- Reinforce programs/promotions

Action Planning (with new leader)
- Set goals
- ESP their team
- Determine development needs
- Establish next week's action plan

Coaching Calls (with aspiring leader)
- Review performance
- Assess progress toward goals
- Motivate/encourage
- Explore new tactics for recruiting and selling
- Target next step

We've covered the secret to turning the flywheel for sustained upward growth. A sales team understands that emotion is really energy and to build performance you must first inspire trust. That involves the soft skills in our business. But hard numbers play a role as well. We may be emotionally driven, but formulas certainly help guide our focus and target where we turn our attention.

Field Segmentation

And that's where we'll turn now – to helpful guides in targeting our attention. The first one I'll share is one that works well when you're in a change environment and you want to gauge where the players sit and what actions to take with each group. Typically in change, a third will shy away. A third will sit on the fence. And a third will embrace the change and get excited about the possibilities. Segmenting your field leaders into three groups based on the characteristics they're showing you, will help determine the right actions to take with each group.

This is the ABC segmentation separating those who may succeed in the new environment, those who are likely to succeed, and those who are unlikely to succeed. The characteristics to help you populate the segments will be both performance as well as attitudes. Once you've placed the leaders where you feel they fall, then it's time to plot the actions.

The "maybe" group are slightly underperforming but have a good attitude. They deserve your full attention on helping them identify leaders on their team and visiting them with workshops and field meetings.

The "highly likely" to succeed team are surpassing performance requirements and have a positive attitude about the future. This is the group you continue with the one on one coaching and action planning. You provide workshop training and field visits.

The last group, the "unlikely to succeed" C group, is underperforming and has expressed in action or attitude they may still be here in body, but have checked out in spirit. They are negative about the future and tend to suck the air out of everyone around them. You don't spend your time here. You let them know you're here when they're ready to go after what they really deserve. Until then, you will respect their space and let their own performance determine how long they stay in the business. Here is a sample format for this kind of segmentation:

Leader Segmentation

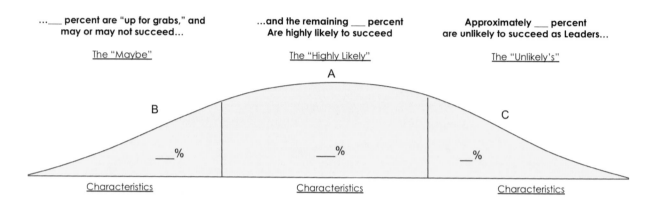

...___ percent are "up for grabs," and may or may not succeed...

The "Maybe"

...and the remaining ___ percent Are highly likely to succeed

The "Highly Likely"

Approximately ___ percent are unlikely to succeed as Leaders...

The "Unlikely's"

A

B

C

___%

___%

___%

Characteristics

Characteristics

Characteristics

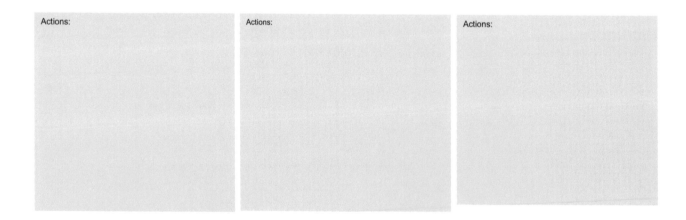

Actions:

Actions:

Actions:

The next kind of segmentation also guides you in where you spend your time, but it's based on volume and growth. It segments your leaders into four groups using an axis to indicate volume and one to indicate percent of growth over last year. Those who fall into the low volume, low growth category will get less of your individualized time. Those in the high volume, high growth will become your primary focus.

The Sales Team as a Team

A sales team must carry the vision, belief and the path. I have found the most effective sales team is a blend of expertise, a diverse and talented group with two factors in common: competence and character. The perfect blend looks like this:

- High Emotional Intelligence.
  - Self aware
  - Socially adept
- Grounded in the direct selling business.
- Strong mix of skills.
  - Business analysis
  - Facilitation and Adult learning
  - Strong communicator
  - Computer skills
  - Socially aware
  - Motivational
- Egoless.
  - The team as a whole is greater than the sum of the individuals.

1. Sales leaders are focused on both relationships and results.

2. Emotions are more than feelings. They're energies.

3. The job of a sales leader is connected to the strategically vital – building sales force count by building field leadership.

4. Sales teams lead people and manage things.

5. A sales team builds trust, commitment, performance and results by being principle-centered.

6. The action that brings the biggest return for a sales team is contact, contact, contact.

7. Field segmentation will show you where and how to spend your time.

8. The ideal sales team is an egoless blend of expertise.

CHAPTER FOUR:

Pink Sky at Night New Seller Start
Roadmaps the first 120 days

Big things come from small beginnings. If, that is, the small beginning is the right beginning.

Over half of direct sellers lost to attrition are lost in their first 13 weeks. No other time in sellers' lives are they more vulnerable and need more "take me by the hand" structure and "at my fingertips" support than they do in those critical first three months. Paying close attention to the first 72 hours, mapping out structure and awards for that first 30 day mark and creating a path to follow with recognition and awards over the next 60 days are smart investments in time and resources. You've likely awarded the recruiter for signing up the recruit so it makes sense you assure yourself a return with an active and engaged new seller.

Assuring yourself an active new seller is just one of the benefits of having a strong New Seller Success System. One study I was involved in showed the faster a new seller makes money, the more she sells and the longer she stays. So a New Seller Success System not only gets a seller active, it also boosts productivity and retention.

New Seller Touch Points

So let's take a look at the aspects of a new seller's life that are critical touchpoints to study when creating a New Seller Success System. With each one, identify your strengths and explore obstacles and missing components in your current new seller experience.

Being approached

- Is there sufficient belief in your opportunity by your current sales force to readily start conversations about your business opportunity?

- What is the perception of your brand and your product by the public at large? Have you taught your sales force to have a 30-second commercial that answers the question, "What do you do"? There is nothing more powerful than having a benefit-driven answer to that question front of mind for your sales force.

- Do you arm your sales force with tools to carry the message for them? Confidence creates conversations.

Registering

- Is sign-up easy and available by phone and online?

- Have you provided your sales force a new recruit hotline? Sometimes a new seller will feel more comfortable providing confidential information to the company over an individual.

- Does your application have an inviting and friendly tone or a legal and foreboding one?

- Is there too big a gap between signing the agreement and receiving business materials? The energy generated by saying yes can be turned into action or doused by doubt when you allow a vacuum to form. Fill the vacuum immediately with information, inspiration and first steps to take.

Getting Started

- Do you have a Business Kit or Package that's inspiring and intuitive?

- Does the act of opening it re-energize the new seller?

- Is making money possible within the first 2 weeks in business?

Making first sale

- Have you given your new sellers confidence to make that first sale?

- Is product training at their fingertips, bite-sized and accessible?

- Do you provide training around marketing yourself as a business owner so making connections with new prospects is easy? Providing business cards, toll-free sizzle messages, e-mail flash presentations, leave-behind post cards, merchandising flyers online, affordable catalogs – these are marketing tools that make a new seller feel confident about tackling that first sale.

- Do you provide limited-time special offers to first X number of customers of a new seller? Having an exclusive benefit to offer as a way to introduce a new business within a limited time, not only makes the new seller feel good about talking, it also encourages quick action.

Recruiting first new seller

- Do you have opportunity messages professionally packaged and easily accessible so new sellers feel confident and proud?

- Are opportunity flyers inside your kit?

- Do you provide the new seller recognition and rewards for recruiting a new team member within their first 30 days? 60 days? 90 days?

Stepping up to first level leadership

- Do you provide a roadmap to move up to your first leadership level?

- Are the benefits of doing so valued and easily understood by a brand new seller?

- Have you branded and packaged the lifestyle of leadership in your company in a presentation that's accessible to your entire sales force?

- Is seeing it or being a part of it included in the established roadmap for a new seller?

Respect the Butterfly Effect.

When it comes to direct selling, it IS where you start! The impact on outcome based on where you start in this business is a bit like the impact discovered by a meteorologist conducting weather experiments. Rather than start the computer back at the beginning of the data trail, he took a short cut and started somewhere in the middle in doing the second round check calculating weather phenomena. The result of the different starting points was dramatic. The same numbers existed in the second half of the data trail; the entry point was the only difference. The results, however, were as different as a sunny day and a Typhoon. This realization of the difference a tiny change can make to the outcome came to be known as the "Butterfly Effect." The name was chosen because a small change like the flap of a buttlerfly's wing on one side of the world could be the trigger to cause a tsunami on the other side of the world. In other words, little things can have big impact. And that little thing could be as simple as the point you put your business into action…the first day it's open or 60 days later.

Design Your System

Study the behavior of your new sellers in their first 120 days. What do they sell in 30 days? How many actually recruit anyone in their first 90 days? What percent step into your first rung of leadership in their first 120 days? Now determine what you would like to see the answers to those questions be. Measure the value of the difference in what is and what you want it to be. Using the value, determine the expenditure you can budget to your New Seller Success System.

In your system, you will fill the gaps you uncovered in your analysis of the touch points of a new seller. You will evolve your Business Kit. You will eliminate vacuums of information and create rewards attached to the behaviors of making that first sale, recruiting that first team member and stepping up to your first leadership level.

So your system will include:

- Step by step training.

- Tools to ease the act of selling, recruiting and moving up.

- An inspiring, intuitive and confidence-building Business Kit.

- And a reward system attached to these behaviors:

- o   Taking action within 72 hours.

- o   Selling a qualifying volume in the first 30 days.

- o   Recruiting within 30 days, 60 days, 90 days.

- o   And moving into leadership within 120 days.

In Review:
Pink Sky at Night New Seller Success System

1. Big things come from small beginnings.

2. Half of direct sellers lost to attrition are lost in their first 13 weeks.

3. Critical time frames in a new seller's life are first 72 hours, first 30 days, first 90 days.

4. The faster a new seller makes money, the more she sells and the longer she stays.

5. There are critical touch points in a new seller's life that require your examination of obstacles and gaps at each one.

6. Analyze current performance of your new sellers in activity, recruiting and leadership development.

7. Set new desired standards in these three areas.

8. Measure the value of the difference.

9. Establish a New Seller Success System budget.

10. Create learning experiences, communication tools, an inspiring and intuitive Business kit and rewards program.

11. Attach rewards to activity, recruiting and moving into leadership.

CHAPTER FIVE:

Pink Sky at Night Recruiting
Attracts your Sales Force

As you know, you are completely dependent on attracting and mobilizing a sales force in order to survive as a direct selling company. That relationship is vital and begins the minute you open your mouth about your company and is impacted by every visual and reference shown to the public and your sales force.

So it's imperative that the act of recruiting is understood and practiced by both corporate executives and field leaders. To build that understanding for successful recruiting requires you to first understand and appreciate how people think. Buyer psychology is the new playing field for a sales team. Selling in the traditional sense is passé, old school, downright dead. Trying to convince someone to sign a new consultant agreement based on facts, figures and a history lesson about your company is about as effective as pushing water up a hill. Memorizing and regurgitating a set sales script will make their eyes glaze over. Putting into play a manipulative closing technique will set off alarms and send them running.

It's not about explaining the compensation plan, the company history or the product manufacturing process. It's not about convincing them the world will continue to turn on its axis if they sign or crash at their feet if they don't. It's not about explaining or convincing at all. It's about connecting, relating, and helping. It's about human motivation. It's about knowing how to start conversations, connecting on a personal level and relating what you hear to what you have. So let's be a student and get to know ourselves a bit better. What can we learn about human motivation?

It seems we're walking billboards. We're sending out messages without saying a word. We just show up and people around us pick up on what's going on inside.

The reason is this. Your heart talks. Literally. Einstein proved that everything is energy. So it seems your emotions are too. Scientists physically can measure the electromagnetic field you produce up to 5 feet away from you. Emotional changes create electrical charges which can be felt by others and measured by scientists. What does that have to do with recruiting?

Well, if you're focused on what's in it for you to get this new team member – the trip you'll win, the extra money you'll make, the recognition you'll get – then your intent on helping yourself will be communicated. The prospect will feel it. He or she may not consciously know why skepticism and fear is building inside, but there is no doubt it is. You become a salesman. And when you convey that image, the feeling that there's a win/lose event ahead sets in. And that feeling will lead to resistance, excuses and an overwhelming desire to escape.

On the other hand, if you enter a business opportunity discussion fully focused on discovering how you can help the person, how you can make a difference, then you're emitting a different message.

You are now a collaborator. You've gone from evoking a feeling you're doing something TO them to the feeling you're doing something FOR them. You're no longer on the opposite side of the table; you're on the same side of the table. You're now a confidant, a friend, a problem solver.

You can fill in the blanks as to the difference being a salesman or being a friend makes in the recruiting conversation. Intent = impact…either good or bad. So check your motivation before you begin conversations. Remember it's not about you. Keep your intent on giving not on getting. You'll feel real; they'll feel relaxed; and your team size will grow.

Fear Blocks

Now here's another bit of prep work for you to consider. There is one overriding emotion that is the ultimate block to recruiting. That emotion is Fear. Fear on the part of recruiters – that they don't know enough or they may be rejected. And fear on the part of the prospect. Fear of risk, fear of looking stupid, fear of not being able to do this business. So how do you tackle fear?

First let's talk from the recruiter's perspective. To conquer fear for the recruiter, remind them that it's not about knowing all the facts and having all the information. It IS about relating. It's about getting to know someone. It's about talking for the purpose of discovering how you can help someone. It's about asking questions. In fact, the best answer to recruiting is always a question. It's about being a problem solver, a dream giver, a friend. So no need to fear the lack of knowledge. You don't need a lot of facts. You simply need to know the benefits of your business so you can pick the ones that match the need or desire you hear. Easy enough.

Next, let's overcome the fear of rejection. Help recruiters understand that "no" simply means the time isn't right for a yes right now. If the recruiter has done her part by matching needs with the benefits of the business, keeping intent on giving instead of getting, responding to objections with the understanding they're natural, they had them too, and found through experience they were unwarranted, then it's time to move to the next phase in the conversation. The phase that keeps the door open.

Simply relate to the fact that timing is everything and timing may not be right at the moment. Then get agreement that things change and because they do, ask permission to check back later. Record the conversation in your lead file and turn your attention to moving on.

Now it's time for the next bit of head work. Time for a little pumping up. So throw yourself a life saver and shift the way you think of the word "NO." Instead of it meaning a dead end, shift it to mean "New Opportunity." Some one is waiting for you, so turn the corner and look for the New Opportunity to help someone with the solutions of your business. Now doesn't that feel better than getting stuck at a dead end?

What's creating fear and blocking recruiting from the prospect's perspective? What lessons from behavioral science can help us overcome self-defeating tendencies on the part of the prospect?

Regret Aversion

We'll start with this one. We're fallible. We're illogical. We're human. And as such, we have some quirks that by knowing them we can overcome them.

For instance, we as humans have more pain around the possibility of losing than we have joy around the possibility of gaining. In a recruiting conversation, you have to know that your prospects are sitting there with this great big aversion to risk pounding in their heads. They fear regretting the decision. They fear losing something important. They fear looking silly. Feeling silly. Failing.

How do you respect this aversion to risk and overcome it at the same time? When you see the discomfort start and the excuses to avoid the risk of doing something, anything at all, creep into the conversation, obliterate the risk by addressing it head on. Get right to it by saying, "So what's the worse that could happen? You get special buying privileges on your products and recoup your investment when you help ___ people (the # based on your averages that would generate the amount of earnings to cover the cost of the entry cost) to the same (product benefits) you're enjoying. That's as bad as it gets, which is not so bad, right?"

Status Quo Bias

Being afraid of risk is just one of the hurdles. Your prospect is also sitting in front of you with a gigantic status quo bias. That simply means people tend to value the way things are over any other choice, even when the choice is clearly preferable. They like it just the way it is. Status quo. Comfey and familiar. So when you're offering a business opportunity and comparing it to a job they may currently have, they're secretly valuing the job because they own that job. It's theirs and therefore, it feels more comfortable than signing up for a new business to replace that job. Even if their boss is a tyrant, their schedule has swallowed them whole, and their paycheck is stuck in 1962. When the choice comes down to action, they hang on to the familiar. They get stuck in the status quo bias.

So what do you do to respect that bias and at the same time overcome it? Here's an idea. Get them to imagine owning your business and living the benefits of it everyday. Paint the picture specifically of how it feels and what it means now that they have this business. Then from this perspective, ask them to choose whether to keep the business they own or take the job that would be new to them. Change the perspective by shifting ownership and the natural tendency toward status quo begins to work in your favor rather than against you.

Pricing and Value

Now here's an interesting human foible that has insight in our business. It's about pricing and value. Two different things entirely. People want value. They demand value. And that doesn't mean deep discounting and basement level pricing strategy. Since this chapter is on recruiting, let's make this discussion of pricing and value apply to your Business Opportunity Kit.

Remember Pulp Fiction? John Travolta and Uma Thurman. He orders a hambuger and cherry soda. She orders a hamburger and $5 Shake. Five dollars, an unheard of price for a drink! Travolta's character got stuck on that price. He became mesmerized by that $5 shake. It must be extraordinary to be worth $5! Finally, he couldn't hold back any longer and asked for a sip of this $5 shake. He had to have a taste!

The message here – don't charge less, sell better. Discounting is not the answer, building value is. Price shoppers will run to the best deal, wherever it is. You want them to stick with you because of the value created out of relationships, service and return on investment. If the shake had been half price, that would have been the end of the conversation. I'm not suggesting you jack the price up as high as you can get it, and expect recruiting to fly off the chart. You have to stay within the acceptable price corridor of your market.

The point is to make the value received for the price higher than expected. Be sure your kit is polished and professional. Pack it with representative product, take-me-by-the-hand training, enticing advertisement of your new seller award program, and a warm, personalized welcome. Hold it up like it's made of gold. Mesmerize them with the value, begin building the relationship, and show them how to get a return on the investment quickly. Like Travolta, you want them feeling that even a sip, a mere taste of your business will be well worth it!

Choice = Collaboration.
Too many Choices = Confusion.

Funny thing happens when it comes to choice. Providing one increases success; providing too many erodes it.

So what does that have to do with recruiting? Let's start with the question of whether or not providing a choice for entry into your business makes sense.

It's been my experience that providing a choice as to how someone opens a business creates a spirit of collaboration between the recruiter and the prospect. Rather than feeling pushed into opening the business on the company's terms, the prospect feels she has some control. The recruiter helps her pick what fits her. They're on the same side with the same mission of doing what works best for the prospect. A standard Business Kit? A higher-end Business Kit? Which is right for you? Now the prospect is evaluating kits rather than rethinking the yes or no decision.

Choice = collaboration = more sign-ups.

But can you have too many choices? According to a study at Princeton University, the answer seems to be yes. Two groups were formed. One was given the choice to buy a Sony appliance for $99 or to wait to learn about other models. Group Two was given the choice to buy the Sony for $99, wait for other models or to buy a different brand for $159. In Group One, the overwhelming majority said they would buy the Sony. In Group Two, nearly half said they wouldn't buy anything. Adding the third choice tipped the scale toward confusion and procrastination, a direct seller's nightmare.

Another study had the same results. A kiosk to sell jam was set up with 24 jams to taste and buy. Another booth was set up with a selection of 6 jams to taste and buy. Thirty percent of those going to the booth with 6 jams made a purchase. Only three percent of those exposed to the selection of 24 jams made a purchase. The more choices, the harder the choice.

So the conclusion for us? Don't overdo a good thing. Providing choice is good; overwhelming your sales force and customers with choice is bad.

Discovery is Key

Discovery is fluid not linear. It's not about lining up a string of facts. It's about flowing through a conversation guided by questions and a spirit of service. Asking questions to people you want to help kicks off discovery.

"How's work today?"

"What's on your child's wish list THIS week?"

"What's missing you'd like to change?"

In other words, have questions that help you discover what people want, need, fear, dream about and wish for. Then turn the conversation to your business with a transition sentence as simple as …

"I may have an answer to (whatever was said), if you're open to it."

Then match the need, concern, dream, or desire you heard to a benefit in the business. It's amazing the difference in interest level when you move from talking TO someone to talking WITH them. Find out what they want – what's beneath the surface – and match it to what you have. You're not here to impress people with how much you know; you're here to bless them with how much you can change their lives.

Moving into the Answer

So the questions created the attraction, now what? Another question, of course. Move into presenting your business by again finding the fit so you can match your answer to their needs. To find out what they truly want from a business like yours, say something like this…

"Some people do what I do because they just love our product and want special buying privileges. Some do what I do because they want a little extra money and have a few hours a week to get it. And some see this as the perfect way to have a business where they call the shots and can make executive-level income. Which one sounds like you?"

Whatever they say is the perfect answer because you're all about matching what you have with what they want –not with a script. If they love the product and simply would like a way to get it cheaper – then show them how smart it is to open a business and get it at consultant cost. Your job will be to introduce new ways to leverage this business after they've taken the first step of registering and getting their business kit.

If they want a little extra money to pay off a credit card, or get something specific, then equate the dollar amount they need to the time it takes to make it. Use averages in your business and let them know these are averages. Your company should know the average customer purchase or if you're a party plan, the average sales per party. Your company should also know the average amount of time to secure the sale or hold the party. With that information and your commission percentage on personal sales, you can share the number of hours a week for the dollar amount they need.

If you have someone before you who sees the real potential of leadership money, then show them all the revenue sources in your business and the roadmap to leadership. Share success stories of other leaders in your company and the amount of time it took to get to that level. This isn't a get rich quick scheme. It's a business that requires focus, commitment and time. You don't have to take a second mortgage to pay for a franchise fee or to set up a retail store. The entry is friendly and doable. The potential is eye-popping. Share both with this aspiring new leader.

Then complete your Discovery Chat by asking how soon they want to start making money. More than likely, "right now" will be the answer. So help them open their business right now!

Build a System

Use systems and build roadmaps. Be clear, simple, and accessible with your recruiting message.

Build your tool kit to include:

- Out and about tools such as
  - Leave-behind postcards that answer the questions:
    - How much can I make?
    - How long does it take?
    - How do I get started?

- A toll-free "sizzle message" for those times your new consultants are lost for words. They simply speed dial the hotline and say, "Take a quick listen and you'll know why I'm so excited about my business."

- A flash presentation that highlights the benefits of your business that can be placed on your email signature and be shared with anyone you meet.

- Teach everyone to have their own 30 second commercial. It is their answer to the question, "What do you do?" Be sure it's a commercial and not a history lesson meaning it highlights the best of the business instead of a linear accounting of when and how you started your business.

- Teach your leaders to develop their own 3-minute "I-story" that shares the difference the business has made for them and their families. The purpose of the "I-Story" is

  - To inspire and mobilize

    - To tell others how your decision made a difference in your life.

    - To get them to act on what they hear

To be effective, your I-story must excite you and it must be easy to follow. That means organizing your thoughts in your choice of a variety of ways:

- Sequential – from opening day to today.

- Categorical – around a theme such as money, time, freedom

- Problem-Solution - starting with a frustration to the solution you found

- Contrast/comparison – the differences in having your own business and being employed in a job, or this business and some other direct selling business.

I've found a helpful guide in getting the power in your story is to use POWER as an acronym to guide you:

- Pop – surprise them with an attention-getting question, visual or story.

- One – stick to one key message

- Windows – provide examples and specifics that give meaning to your message

- Everyday language – speak conversationally

- Retention line – end with a memorable line or thought that punctuates your main message.

However you started the conversation with a prospect – with a question, 30 second commercial or your I-story, you bridge to the rest of the story with a transition question such as, "What's the best thing you've heard so far?"

Then move into your Discovery Chat that's guided by the questions you saw earlier:

Some open a business for the buying privileges. Some for a little extra money. Some for the big money. Which sounds good for you?

And remember, whichever answer they give, customize your response to focus on that benefit. If they want the product at special consultant prices, focus on the discount and the money to be saved. If they need a little extra money, focus on the flexible schedule and the return on time in your business. If the big money is of interest at this point, go right to the leadership advantages and examples of those who've turned the business into big income.

Be fluid, be relaxed, be relevant. Remember, it's a "discovery" chat not a dissertation.

A Recruiting System Includes:

Out and About Tools	Grab intrerest	Focus on Benefits
30 Second Commercial & 3 minute I-Story	Benefit-driven commercial	Personlize the benefits
Questions and Discovery Chat	Move the conversation from interest to information	Customize benefits to fit needs/desires

Pink Sky at Night Recruiting

1. Buyer psychology is the new playing field for direct sellers.

2. Your intent is the key to your impact on others. Focus on giving rather than getting.

3. A flexible and dynamic approach built on questions you match to the business enhances results.

4. Fear of failure or making a mistake is a driving emotion for prospects.

5. Success is not about remembering and repeating a script; it's about relaxing and relating to your prospect.

6. NO means "New Opportunity."

7. Learn from Behavioral Science to counter Regret Aversion and Status Quo Bias and to exploit the attraction to value.

8. Providing choice is good; overwhelming your sales force and consumers with it is bad.

9. Build a recruiting system that provides a track to guide your sales force.

CHAPTER SIX:

PINK SKY AT NIGHT COMMUNICATIONS, EDUCATION, EVENTS & RECOGNITION
Mobilize your Sales Force

Ernst & Young did a study to determine the importance investors place on non-financial measures. The conclusion of the study? The study showed that 1/3 of a stock's share price can be attributed to non-financial matters. Matters like innovation, strategy execution and management credibility. Non-financial matters that revolve around people --alive, spirited and mobilized people.

So in this chapter, the focus turns from attracting people to your business to awakening their spirits and energizing their commitment. This people business of ours is not a still portrait. It is a kaleidoscope of color, of ever-changing goals and emotions. Of people helping people live better lives. Our compelling reason for being.

So how do we create the environment for this kind of noble purpose? How do we energize and mobilize people to live their best lives?

We use the people-building tools of this business. Communications, Education, Events and Recognition. Together these disciplines should be strategically focused, linked to one another, and built for the purpose of nurturing relationships, expanding possibilities and inspiring trust.

So let's start with Communications.

Here are top tips gathered from experience in both the doing and the refining and the re-doing of communications for direct sellers.

1. Give it to them straight – the good, bad and ugly. In other words, communicate openly and honestly. Don't fall prey to watering down the message to avoid an uncomfortable topic. I was asked to do that kind of watering down many years ago which led me to write this poem in frustration of weasel words:

Tip, tip, tip on my tippy toes

Up here safe where nobody knows

Where I stand or where this goes

I'm covering this ground on my tippy toes

   So address the message head on with candor and rationale and you won't have to be reminded of the 'tippy toe" poem.

2. Tell them "why" before how or what.

3. Silence is NOT golden especially in times of change. The rumor mill cranks up at full speed when there is a vacuum of information. Communicate often from all angles.

4. Punctuate the good news with celebration and consistency. In times of change emphasizing the good that's happening is critical. People want to be a part of success, so be sure everyone knows what's working. If you meet a goal or make a number, shout it from the rooftops. Then watch folks climb on board!

5. Protect their time as the most precious resource. Give your leaders "Executive Summaries" so they get the big picture in short order. Provide them search-driven and intuitive online environments. Give your leaders presentation–ready launches with speaker notes so they're not spending time creating paperwork. They're focused on people-work instead.

6. Avoid random acts of chaos. Knee-jerk reactions creating inconsistent news flying at the field sporadically causes frustration and confusion. Establish a news day and stick to it.

7. Leverage technology. Using podcasts, audio links online, blogs, My-Space profiles of events, YouTube videos promoting your opportunity, products or events – this Wild West of communications is fun, relevant and accessible. Mix it up and try it out!

8. Reach out and touch their hearts with targeted milestone communications. A welcome letter to a new Consultant, congratulatory note from the Sales leader at each new career level, an action plan and encouragement to an aspiring leader, a personal card and call to a new leader from top executives, flowers and a feature story on leaders who advance to top levels—these are examples of milestone communications. Make them personal and you'll make them powerful.

9. Create unfiltered feedback directly from the field to top executives. Keeping your finger on the pulse of the sales force is critical to staying relevant and on-target. The Ten-Point Feedback Loop here will guide you in designing topics for consultation with your Feedback Board.

Your Feedback Forum...

Reading the Pulse & Providing Sales Force Intelligence

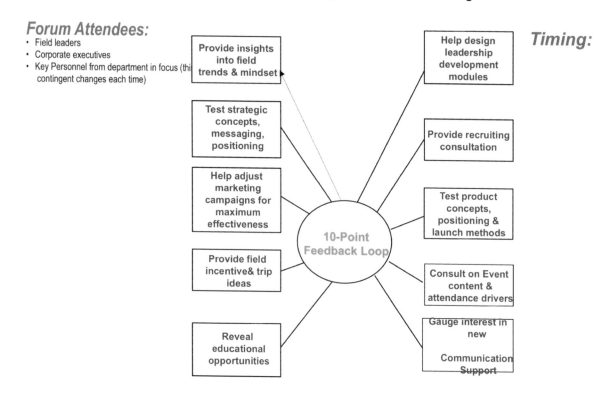

Forum Attendees:
- Field leaders
- Corporate executives
- Key Personnel from department in focus (this contingent changes each time)

Provide insights into field trends & mindset

Test strategic concepts, messaging, positioning

Help adjust marketing campaigns for maximum effectiveness

Provide field incentive& trip ideas

Reveal educational opportunities

10-Point Feedback Loop

Help design leadership development modules

Provide recruiting consultation

Test product concepts, positioning & launch methods

Consult on Event content & attendance drivers

Gauge interest in new Communication Support

Timing:

Education & Development

I've often thought you train animals and teach people, so I've morphed the "Training" designation to "Education and Development." This is where the magic happens in a direct selling company. People are taken from sitting on their hands to dancing and expanding and becoming their wild, wonderful selves. The journey begins with "take me with you" learning for new sellers all the way through elevated leadership development focused not on who leaders are in title but on who they are inside.

Every step of your career plan should have a learning module devoted to it. If you have a gap in learning, you'll have a gap in confidence and a gap in confidence leads to a dip in sales.

The goal of your Chief Learning Officer is to link not only steps in your career path, but also your mission critical focus to learning opportunities. Recruiting, activation, leadership development – these are mission critical and should have focused tactics devoted to each one.

And speaking of linking, it's imperative that all departments in a direct selling company participate first hand in the learning opportunities provided by Education and Development. Keeping the training team and tactics integral to all the other disciplines in the company will assure strategy is understood and the actions we encourage our sales force to take are supported company wide.

Just as in all areas, how people learn and want to be reached is changing rapidly with the evolution of technology. Here are a few learning trends influencing the way you deliver content and reach people:

Learning Trends

1. People want "fingertip knowledge." They want accessible and convenient learning opportunities.

2. People want to learn in "chunks." They want it given to them in bite-size pieces.

3. Social networks have created the "wisdom of the crowds" phenomenon. Blogs, chatlines, message boards, and Wikkis are attractive.

4. People expect fast and quick delivery methods. They want an easy search and a thorough choice of content.

5. People enjoy a blended approach to learning.

    a. Self-study guides

    b. Self-paced e-learning

    c. Expert networks

    d. Webinars

e.　Podcasts

6.　And taking a holistic approach to learning is a growing trend. Teaching the whole person is more than covering the mechanics of the business. It includes

　　　a.　Values

　　　b.　Emotional/Social issues

　　　c.　Physical/Mental Health

　　　d.　Intellectual growth

Getting Unstuck

Have you ever bought a picture frame with that nasty little sticker on the glass? The glue that's holding that sticker could easily hold a building together. You could build a bridge with that glue. That stuff is tough. But when you put a little Goo-Be-Gone lubricant on it, the sticker gets unstuck. What seemed to be cemented in place is now moving right off the glass. Pretty amazing. And so is the work of Education and Development. It's like that Goo-Be-Gone lubricant. Apply a little to your sales force and watch them get unstuck and moving right along.

So be sure you have a strong and complete Education and Development strategy built around…

- Your Mission Critical focus on recruiting, activation and leadership development

- Targeted career levels with a success plan for each

- Reinforcement of your programs, promotions and products

- Workshops built around main drivers for your Sales Team to Deliver

- New Leadership Orientation

- Advanced Leadership Events

- Continuing Education online, in print and at events

Special Events

Group dynamics builds momentum in our business. The benefits of recognition and relationships are exponential in a group setting. Attitudes are contagious and emotions are amped up when people are shoulder to shoulder. So ask yourself when reviewing your event schedule, how will this make them FEEL? Your schedule for your event is not about function; it's about feeling.

Do you remember the movie, City Slickers? The old crusty cowboy character played by Jack Palance kept Billy Crystal's character wondering throughout the movie what the "one thing" to life was. He said simply, "There's one thing. The secret to life is just one thing." And then he rode off in the sunset.

Well, you can rent the movie if you want to know the movie's answer. As far as "the one thing" to a successful event, here it is...

It's not what happens on the stage or the page; it's what happens in the hearts of the giver and receiver that matters.

Simple on the surface, but let your mind roll around in this "one thing" a bit more before moving on. First take a moment considering the heart of the giver – in other words, the intent of the presenter on stage. The presenter's intent has to be selfless and focused on the audience. Presenters must feel confident that what they're giving to the audience is important and in their best interest. Anything less than this kind of belief, sincerity and egoless presentation will feel stuffy and detached to the audience. And you've just spent precious resources in time and money on the preparation and delivery. What a waste.

Now think for a minute about the heart of the receiver. Well, here's the true measure of your success. Did trust and commitment grow as a result of the event experience? Or did they walk away thinking about the money they just spent? When you left your event, where did you leave the hearts of your attendees?

Naturally, you're hoping it's with trust and commitment. A successful event is not about logistics; it's about human connection.

So how do you map out an Event for that kind of response in the hearts of your attendees? Here is a guide I've found will frame a successful event:

- Make an impression. There is nothing more lasting than a first impression, so make yours about more than entertainment. Make those first few moments sing your respect for the audience, your appreciation of their attendance, and the huge return they'll enjoy from being there.

- Immerse your attendees in every aspect of your business – from product innovations to income generation. Literally wrap the experience around them by surrounding them in thematic color and benefit-driven signage, involve them in entertainment, tour them through your home office or manufacturing facility, step them into bite-sized learning booths, recognize them in private networking parties.

- Engage them onstage, in learning, and in your leadership career path by pulling them into openings and closings, taking recognition out in the house for field leaders to congratulate and present at their tables, providing pledge cards and dream-signing boards. Attendees want interaction. Allow them to co-create the experience.

- Connect them with top field leaders and your support tools and programs. Connect holistically by relating to more than the mechanics of the business. Connect with their values, their minds, their spirits and their hearts. Remember, you're not there to inform. You're there to inspire. If they want to be informed, they can read the newspaper.

- Focus them on achieving a short-term challenge when they get home which will help them step up into leadership. Keep your "Learning Day" focused on the strategically vital and taught by the best of the best. Spotlight success stories by allowing top performers to share the "what and how" throughout your event.

- Counteract BS detectors by making sure your presenters know their scripts well enough to speak them and not read them. The tone should be conversational and natural. Consider replacing scripts with bulleted reminders of key points which force the presenter toward more natural conversation.

- Close with power. The closing of your event is the last impression you make. Be sure that impression is attached to your mission critical focus and builds toward sustainable growth and not merely a momentary spike.

Opportunity-Focused Events

Outside in Perspective

Create Memories so Trust & Commitment Grow

Field Stories

Field Participation

Field Focus opening to close

Focused

- Intersperse tools and launches throughout with a focused recruiting challenge near close.

- Be sure your "takeaway" idea is "connected to moving up on your career path. Literally move the audience with interactive device connected to moving up and growing

Connected

- **Connect** to the values of audience providing powerful memorable moments.

- Sprinkle field leadership talks throughout event connecting their personal stories to audience

- Provide numerous opportunities to **"step into" the picture** with mirrors, photo ops, sign -on boards, booths.
- Open sessions with video or live testimonials that connect and inspire attendees.

Engaged

- Involve your future leaders in **openings** so they become participants rather than observers.

- Recognize large #'s with a **touch of intimacy** by asking Leaders to hand award to team at tables.
- Pull achievers into

  entertainment acts

- Honor Recruiters and developers in special qualification events /dinners/parties.

- **Allow** attendees to literally walk inside all aspects of the business in booths and expo-like venues.

Immersed

One word to describe an opportunity -focused event: **"immersion."**

Literally wrap your experience around attendees by
1. surrounding them with color,
2. involving them in entertainment,
3. stepping them into bite-sized learning,
4. recognizing them in networking parties & audience activities.

And Don't Forget Follow-up

Following up with your attendees with a thank you note and an overview or recap of the event is a great way to show appreciation and prepare for next year's success.

And an imperative step in follow up is the debrief with selected attendees and your production team. You want to tackle each phase of the event and determine what you would retain as is, what you need to refine for next year, what needs a drastic overhaul, and what you would eliminate entirely. The next form serves as a useful guide to this discussion.

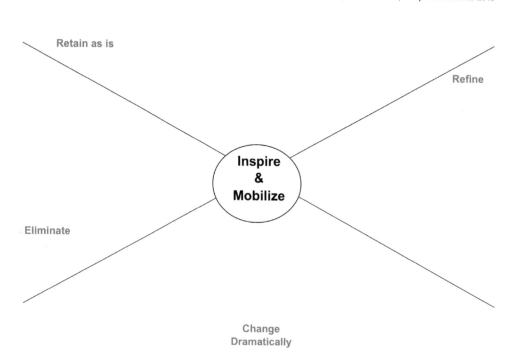

Debrief: Event breakout: Recognize 20%, Inform 10%, Educate 50%, Keep Dream Alive 20%

Retain as is

Refine

Inspire & Mobilize

Eliminate

Change Dramatically

Make Them Feel Important

I once learned from a brilliant leader that to truly connect with someone, you should imagine they have four words written on their foreheads. Those four words are these: Make me feel important.

That's the essence of a successful event for a sales force. They walk away feeling valued and ready to make the next steps in their business. You've made more than memories. You've made new muscle in your business. Your attendees are now competent and confident thanks to your successful event. Congratulations!

Recognition

Maslow's Hierarchy of Needs is a human motivation theory over 50 years old and yet it is still one of the most cited. Well, when addressing recognition, I couldn't resist but cite it once more. Maslow's theory is based on deficiency needs and growth needs.

Recognition plays in the growth needs arena. The need to belong, to affiliate with others and be accepted. This need must be fulfilled before progressing to the next growth need. The need for self-esteem--to achieve and to gain approval.

The social dynamics of our business is a natural place to fulfill the growth needs to belong and build self esteem. Celebrating career level achievements with recognition pins, name badge designations, chair covers, special seating, honor receptions and career level learning events are great ways to create that feeling of affiliation, acceptance and achievement.

By fulfilling those growth needs, your leaders can progress to the ultimate growth areas of self-actualization and self-transcendence. Self-actualization simply means becoming your best. Self-transcendence means going beyond yourself, beyond ego to help others realize their best.

In our business, these two at the top of Maslow's Hierarchy are inherent and natural. Becoming your best is built into career advancement and leadership learning. And reaching out to others, well, the structure of the business itself makes it clear you get ahead by putting other people first. Maslow would look upon direct selling and be pleased.

So our jobs when it comes to recognition, is to align our actions with this well-established hierarchy of human motivation. Here are a few tips I've found that will fulfill the need to belong, to become your best; and help others do the same:

- Little things can make a big impact.

    o A personalized welcome note on the pillow of an event attendee or trip qualifier.

    o The top performer's favorite song playing when he/she is introduced.

    o Having a top field leader introduce an aspiring leader lends prestige, acceptance, honor and camaraderie to the introduction.

- Immediacy matters.

    o Don't let a week go by after a leadership level has been met before you acknowledge it.

    o Give weekly praise.

    o Mark progress toward a big goal with a trinket that connects to the big goal or award.

- Make it personal.

    o Pictures on billboards down the hallways of your events.

    o A choice of awards to fit every personality.

    o Hand delivered gifts named and signed.

    o Surprise your top performer by flying in his/her family as the final tribute in a recognition event.

- Have an audience.

    o Remember the best recognition is done in front of one's peers. Never forget the power of standing out in front of thousands of your best friends.

Recognition is powerful and natural in our business. To be "Maslow-approved," connecting with their hearts is a must-have. Connecting with their values is a must-have. And connecting them with tangible gifts is a nice-to-have. Don't let the story be about the diamond or the trip or the cash bonus. The story is about the evolution of the person who earned it. Exalt their growth and applaud the difference it's made in others. That's recognition at ITS best.

CHAPTER SEVEN:

Pink Sky at Night Leadership
Fuels Growth

Whether you're a leader inside the corporate walls or an independent leader building your own business, this chapter speaks directly to you. It's last in this book, but first in your priorities for pink skying the night and setting the stage for your success.

Leadership is so often talked about and so rarely realized. You see, it's not about who you are in title, but about who you are inside. It's an inside-out game. It starts by looking inward – and mastering your best self. Of course, it's more than staring at your navel. You can't do that forever because success is not self-made. It's team-made. And that requires a leader to not only carry the vision, but to carry the path as well. A leader must reach out with focused discipline and lead the way for others to follow.

So looking in and reaching out will provide the frame for this chapter. Let's get started by examining what's required to "look in."

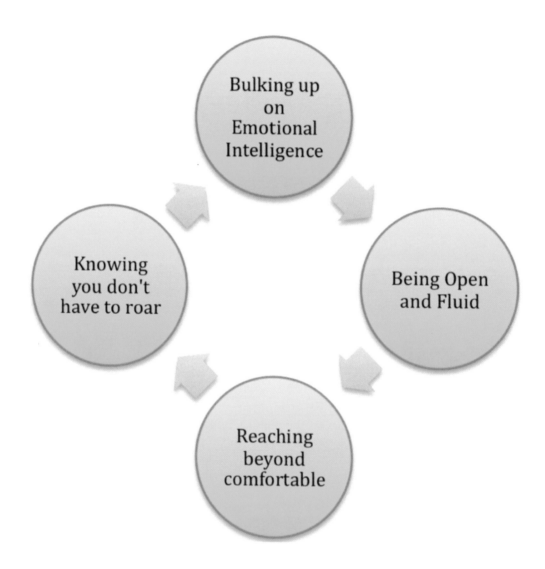

Bulking Up on Emotional Intelligence

Emotional intelligence has proven to be the factor that determines a leader's success two to one over any other factor. Over intelligence. Over experience. Over gender. Over personality. Eighty-five percent of top performers are high in EQ. Studies have compared companies with leaders high in emotional intelligence with those who aren't. Those companies with leaders high in EQ outperformed their counterparts every time.

So what is it? What is emotional intelligence and how do you get it? Well, it's not how much you know. It's not how you act. It's who you are. It's being self-aware, self-managing and socially adept. Let's take a closer look…

Self-aware:
Knowing what you stand for, your strengths, weaknesses, values, and goals.

Self-management:
Making the most of any situation and taking responsibility for your role in the interaction.

Socially adept:
Knowing how to relate successfully with others – picking up emotional cues, managing through conflict and meeting the needs of a relationship.

Remember, leadership is an inside-out game. And being self-aware is the first step in building muscle here. So let's spend some time on this point.

One of my favorite definitions of leadership is the perfect way to start our inner exploration. The definition comes from an extraordinary leader, Colin Powell. He said leadership is "the art of accomplishing more than the science of management says is possible."

I love that! It's an art. It's intangible. It's illusive. We've all seen examples when we've shaken our heads and asked how could that be. When a person with no arms or legs plays the drums or a mother of small frame lifts a 200 pound weight off a fallen child. Science would suggest it's impossible. But it happens. What is that illusive, intangible "art" that accomplishes more than science would say is possible?

The best way I can dig into this answer is to draw from personal experience when I saw the intangible at work. My oldest son, Adam, was always the smallest boy on the team when he was growing up. Any team and every team. It was true grit that got him a place on a travel hockey team. All padded up he was as wide as he was tall. But he hit the ice and forgot his size. He would skate into those corners with guys a helmet size taller and mix it up! He would enter a face-off looking right into the chest of his opponent and come out with the puck. Now that just shouldn't happen. Power on the hockey rink typically means muscle and physical dominance. But not with Adam. At the end of the season his coach called him up in front of his team. He put his arm on his shoulder and said the words that sum up how "art" can beat out "science." He said, "Adam may not be the biggest guy on the team, but I would take a whole team of Adams because he has the heart of a tiger."

The heart of a tiger.

It starts right there, who you are inside, not who you are in size or title. To be a leader, you must have the heart of a tiger …that illusive strength that makes you bigger on the inside than you are on the outside. It's like the story of the little girl who had a cotton candy as big as the top half of her body. When her father looked down and asked with concern if she could eat it all. The little girl looked up and said, "Don't worry, Daddy, I'm bigger on the inside than I am on the outside." Leaders have to be bigger on the inside than they are on the outside.

How well acquainted are you with your inner self? Have you mapped out what you believe to be your mission on this earth? As a parent? As a leader?

This is pretty heavy stuff, I know, but it's the heavy lifting necessary to become a strong leader. For me, my mission as a parent is to raise two principle-centered, independent, joyful young men. As a leader, my mission is to open minds, expand hearts and release greatness in others.

What is your mission? Give yourself the precious gift of taking the time to process this and write down your answer. Your mission will be your frame to guide your leadership. It will be the energy to get over the bumps. It will prioritize your time, put fire in your gut and help you bulk up on emotional intelligence.

After all, you can't reach out and lift someone up if you're not standing on higher ground. You're carrying the vision and seeing the big picture. People are depending on you to inspire them and help them discover the best in themselves. So get in touch with the best in you. This is not syrupy "sweetness and light." This is the stuff that defies science and leaves them shaking their heads and marveling at the results. Remember, soft skills turn into hard numbers. So do your homework:

- Know your values.
- State what you stand for.
- Describe how you want to be remembered.
- Establish your measure of success as a leader, a parent, a human being.

Being Open and Fluid

The next step in "looking in" is to examine your tolerance for change. We all know change is as certain as the sun rising in the East, so why are so many reluctant to embrace it? You may have heard the saying, "You can't step into the same river twice." That sums up the situation. The river is constantly flowing and changing so it's impossible for you to encounter the same river the second time you approach it. Same with the world around us. It's changing so fast it's a blur. So don't expect to approach it like you did yesterday. The world is fluid so you must be too. Decide you're going to become a champion of change. You will expect it and celebrate it. You will reward change agents and strip status quo of its power. You will give those driving change bigger budgets and favored positions. And as the leader, you will sell the dream. You will help those around you see the invisible by giving your vision excitement, drama and glory.

Reaching Beyond the Comfortable

When I was growing up I had a horse which I rode to my friend's house several days a week after school. Now my friend lived less than a half mile away, so the junket was an easy one. When we got there, I would jump down and chat with my friend while my horse grazed on the grass. One day, I decided I wanted to ride past my friend's house. What do you think my horse did? He stopped where he was used to stopping. He refused to go one step past what had become a comfortable routine.

I'm reminded of that often when it comes to leadership. It's easy to get used to just getting by. To settle. To make do. The problem with mediocrity is when you set your eyes on it, you're drawn to it. So if you set your sights on minimums, on the comfortable spot you've gone a hundred times before, what's going to happen? You'll stop when you get there. Adequate becomes the end game. Survival the driving force.

Not fun. Not inspiring. Not the place for a leader. The job of a leader is to reach so high you get dizzy. You see, others are watching, and when you reach, so do they.

I had the experience to see this firsthand. The leaders who signed up for a growth program averaged three times the stretch than those who didn't sign up. All those who signed up didn't necessarily reach their ultimate goal, but they did enjoy the fruits of the stretch. They knew the goal was big but their passion was bigger. That passion was not only big, it was contagious. It started a fire on the team which ignited dreams and transformed mediocrity into greatness.

So it wasn't about the end result. It was about the reach itself and the "becoming" in the process. It's the responsibility of the leader to give that example. To stretch the dream rather than dumbing it down. So find a stretch and go for it.

Knowing You Don't Have to Roar

Possibly you remember the "dress for success" style guide. The power suit, the proper pumps, the tucked and tailored pin striped uniform of an executive who depended on looks to demand attention and command respect.

Well, today there's a new style guide. It's about looking like you belong no matter where you find yourself. It's about fitting in while standing out. Being casual if casual is the dress of the day while expressing a touch of uniqueness -- a touch of color or style that communicates you're not a cookie cutter bore.

But this really isn't about fashion. It's about going deeper than the clothes you wear. It's about projecting a quiet assurance that comes from confidence, competence and real strength. It's about projecting calmness and grace that will earn you real power. The same kind a lion has. He doesn't have to roar, after all, to gain respect. Neither do you.

I've had the great fortune to have worked with top leaders in a variety of direct selling companies. I discovered they were more alike than different, even when the product line was vastly different. Four commonalities stood out as the actions that took them all the way to the top.

Putting Other People First

Here is a leadership truth: It's not about you.

If you try to make it about you, your intent will show. You'll reek of ego and hidden agendas. No one will follow. You'll look around and find you're alone. They've all headed in different directions. Any direction but the one you're walking toward. Obviously, not productive.

If your business is going flat, examine your motivation for leading. Is it to get a promotion? A raise? Career level advancement?

If it is, you've stripped the spirit right out of your business. Profit fluctuations are the direct result of how people feel. Performance and shareholder value depend on emotions and attitudes. The leader sets the tone. And that tone is set by your intent, your motivation for leading.

And this brings me to the first commonality among top leaders – they know this truth. They know their purpose as a leader is to understand their gifts and their meaning as a leader is to give those gifts away. When they put other people first is when they infuse their team with energy, trust and performance.

In every leadership level in a direct selling company whether in the field or at the corporate office, the only real way to get ahead is to focus your efforts on helping others realize their potential. Value relationships as much as you value results and an amazing thing happens. You'll be rewarded with both.

Practicing Consistency

The next shared action of leaders who elevated their leadership and grew to the top in their companies was to practice consistency. There was nothing sporadic or hit and miss about their calendars. If they had a recruiting event the second Tuesday of the month, you could bet on the fact they would have one the second Tuesday of next month, and the month after that. If they had new seller orientation on Monday night, they had it every Monday night. If coaching calls were held with their new leaders, those calls had a permanent place in time and day on their calendars. Their consistency gave their team a reliable track to run on which built momentum over time.

In addition to being consistent about the support they provided their team, they were also consistent about their personal business. Success habits were way-of-life habits. Recruiting, holding leadership interviews, selling product – these success habits were exactly that – habits. They knew that small things done consistently have big impact. One top leader had a habit of stacking up all her order forms and calling ten a day. She became the top in the company. Another leader at the very top of the career level in her company still held parties. Not for the income of the party, but to meet people and find her next leader. Last I checked, she had an $18 million dollar organization. Consistency pays.

Keeping it Simple

This shared practice of keeping it simple is a product of good old common sense. Which is better in our business – to be one of a kind? Or to be one in a million? Both sound pretty good, but the reality is you want to be one in a million people modeling the behaviors that will be passed on to others who will pass them on to others and so on. You want a million repeater stations.

Okay, a million is an exaggerated number, but the point is this. The more people you teach quickly to do what you do, the more money you will make. A "see one-do one" simplicity to your business will give it an "I can do that" attraction and a natural multiplier effect. And that's the kind of math that will have you on your way to building a strong sales force.

- So the simpler your selling method, the better.
- The simpler your recruiting proposition, the better.
- The simpler your new seller orientation, the better.
- The simpler your mentoring system, the better.

The simpler it all is, the quicker it's picked up and handed down making the mentoring process work like a charm.

The mentoring process is the "pass it on" engine of your business. It is the same whether you're teaching the selling method, the recruiting talk, a new seller's entry class, or a workshop to develop leaders. The process consists of five steps to have the multiplier effect. These five steps were inspired by John Maxwell's Five "M's" of mentoring. Essentially the actions are these:

1. You lead by example by doing the action.
2. You do the action and someone is with you to whom you explain the steps and the why behind each one.
3. Then that person does the action and you're with her/him. You provide feedback by saying what you liked best and would do differently next time.
4. Then your someone does the action alone.
5. And finally the cycle begins over when your someone models the action for someone else to learn.

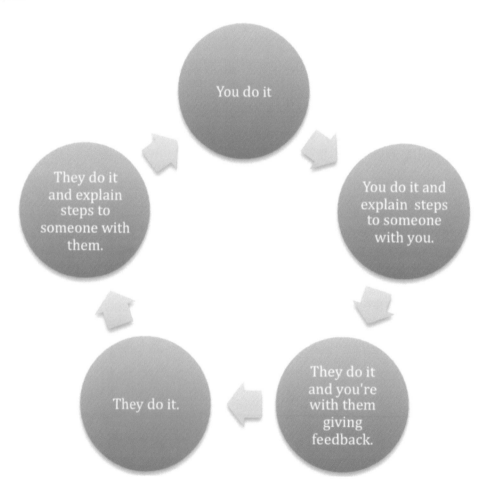

This cycle that builds duplication is dependent on having simple systems in your business. Everyone is following the same system so all meetings and learning opportunities reinforce the same message.

Giving it Enough Time

The fourth lesson that all those leaders shared who made it to the top was this: They learned to give it enough time.

Our business is based on entrepreneurial time, not corporate time. It reminds me of that heart rock my son gave me. Time played an important role. Years of rain, sand, and wind chipped away at the surface carving that perfect heart. The heart was in there all the time, but there was a process that took time to reveal itself.

Our business is that way. You start as an independent contractor and may not make the hourly return right away that you want. In a job—you make that hourly wage – from hour one. That's corporate time. Of course, you're making that same hourly wage a year later. That's corporate time too. But in entrepreneurial time, if you keep applying the force, you chip away at what is hiding your dream. Then finally, you're paid so much more than you could ever imagine. You could have stayed in that corporate job and made a three percent annual increase. Or you take advantage of entrepreneurial time, stick to it, and turn that hourly wage on its head. It would seem unbelievable to talk about a field leader's hourly return to a brand new seller on day one. But a funny thing happens as an independent direct seller. When you divide, you multiply. When you divide your team into new teams with new leaders you've mentored, your income multiplies. And that's when the joy of entrepreneurial time kicks in. You're working the same hours, you're just getting more people to contribute to the return on those hours. The secret to the joy is to stay in the game for the long run and to realize the counterintuitive reality that in our business when you divide your team by promoting new leaders from it, you multiply your income. Sweet.

Pink Sky Leaders are WILD

One of my favorite books growing up was *Call of the Wild* by Jack London. It was all about relationships, loyalty, grit, leadership, love, and dogs. I value all those and have found them to be important in my life. The "call of the wild" meant for me the love of animals. I own three dogs, grew up with a horse, and adopted another horse for a therapeutic riding center. This "call" has merged with my experience as a direct seller to leave lessons I consider to be the best I could pass along to other leaders.

I believe leaders, successful leaders, will always have a wild side. They will never be trapped by self-imposed limitations. They will always break out of scarcity cages and into the freedom of abundance. They will open up to what's around the corner, let go of their fears, laugh loudly and often, and embrace themselves to be fully who they are. They will be wild.

So I would like to leave you with my best advice when it comes to leadership. Take a lesson from the "call of the wild" and be full of

Wonder,
Inspiring,
Loud in your vision and
Delicious in your spirit.

Be WILD!

Wonder Full

Being full of wonder is a precious gift to give yourself. You see things you would never see if you let yourself fall into the jaded, rolling-eyes response. See things as if they're brand new, as if it's your first time. It's the difference between flying through holiday cards in the midst of shopping, wrapping, decorating, cooking and doing all your normal thousand things in the month of December, and taking your holiday cards out on the beach the following July. You'll see so much more than you did in December. Being full of wonder is about being in the moment with a focused attention on the now. Living in the present being open and fully aware. There is nothing more precious than now when you're living full of wonder. It will make every experience powerful and every person the only person.

Inspiring

You've probably picked up this next point in this book by now. I'm a real believer that motivation not legislation will move people forward. Rules will never be the reason someone follows you. What will be the reason is how closely you connect with their inner most desires, concerns, dreams, hopes, wishes, fears. Leadership is not about power. It's about empowerment…which simply means connecting with the dreams of others and the inner strength they have in fulfilling those dreams. That's when you inspire. When you get inside, beneath the suit, beneath the fear, and discover greatness. The word "inspire" originally meant, "breathe." That's what you do when you inspire. You breathe life into dreams.

Loud in your vision

A leader's voice must be heard above the noise of the everyday. Leaders carry the vision, the belief and the path. Speak it out. Be obvious about your goals and desires. Share them with your family, friends, and colleagues. You must shine with certainty so others find their way through you. One of my favorite songs as a child was "This little light of mine, I'm going to let it shine." Remember that one? It reminds me we must let our lights shine as leaders. Not for the purpose of putting ourselves in the spotlight, but for the purpose of shining the light on someone else. Be loud in your vision so you light the way for others.

Delicious in spirit

And finally, a leader must be delicious in spirit. You must attract people to you for what they can gain from being around you. You're like honey. No one can resist because of the sweet gifts they receive when they're with you. This is the law of the harvest. When you give, you receive. So give without expecting anything in return. That's when you will attract people to come into your life, money to flow back to you, and enjoy the delicious rewards of a delicious spirit.

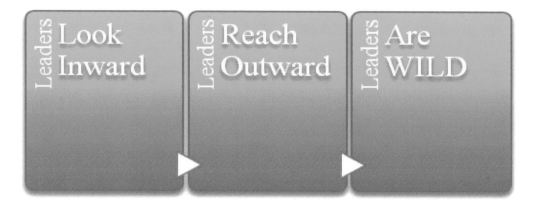

In Review:
Pink Sky Leadership

1. Leadership is not about who you are in title. It's about who you are inside.
2. Leadership starts by looking inward – mastering your best self.
3. Looking inward means bulking up on emotional intelligence, being open and fluid to change, reaching beyond the comfortable, and projecting a quiet assurance that earns real power.
4. Leadership grows by reaching outward carrying the path for others to follow.
5. Reaching out means putting other people first, practicing consistency, keeping it simple and giving it enough time.
6. Pink Sky at Night Leaders are WILD – full of Wonder, Inspiring, Loud in their vision and Delicious in their spirits.

CONCLUSION

There was a horse originally named Midnight who came from a bloodline having three Triple Crown winners. He should have been magnificent on the racetrack. But he wasn't. As a result, his owners saw no value in him and left him to literally fade away and die.

But instead of losing his life, he actually found it. A therapeutic riding facility in Shreveport, Louisiana rescued him. And his real story began. The story of Midnight and a little girl who thanks to one another, each discovered greatness.

The little girl was born with a chromosomal disorder and her parents were told she would never speak or walk. Then when she was five, the family discovered therapeutic riding. Overcoming fear and physical struggle, this little girl got on the back of a horse. Then it happened. She spoke. And the first word she spoke was the name of the horse she was riding. She's been riding ever since. And now she rides the horse with the Triple Crown bloodline and failed racing career. She has given him value again. And he has given her strength. His story now matters not because he stood in the Winner's Circle, but because he walks for a higher purpose. And not because of his regained strength, but because of the strength he's released in the little girl on his back.

That's the essence of Pink Sky at Night success. It's created from both giving and receiving. From spirit and strength. From the illusive and the tangible. From dreams and drivers. From hearts and minds. From math and emotions. From art and science.

Appreciate the duality of pink skying your business and enjoy a new day, a bright day.

LESSONS LEARNED –
ONE FOR EVERY YEAR OF LEARNING

1. Our business is math and emotions wrapped in the minds and hearts of people.

2. Meeting sales goals and profit targets are a direct result of how people feel.

3. If you're nimble instead of numb, you can bend the culture so you protect the company.

4. To lift others, you have to stand on higher ground.

5. Leaders don't settle for sameness; they stretch themselves silly.

6. Emotions are amped up when people are standing shoulder to shoulder.

7. Your recognition story should not be about the prize, but about the evolution of the person who earned it.

8. Value relationships as much as you value results, and you'll be rewarded with both.

9. Rules will never be the reason someone follows your lead.

10. Leadership comes from being quiet in assurance and loud in vision.

11. Recruiting is structured by questions, guided by service and perfected by matching what you hear to what you have.

12. Leaders get ahead by putting other people first.

13. Choice = good; too many choices = bad.

14. It's not what happens on the stage or on the page; it's what happens in the hearts of the giver and receiver that matters.

15. The fire of growth burns hottest in the center of a pocket of passion, the source of which is an aspiring leader.

16. In our business emotions are more than feelings; they're energies that either suck the air out of plans or propel them forward.

17. Your ideal team is an egoless blend of expertise.

18. Those who elevate their view see the depth of what's possible.

19. If you're fixated on now, you may be blind-sighted by next.

20. Good communicators tell it to them now and tell it to them straight.

21. Leaders shape their future from a front row seat. Staying close to the field keeps your vision clear.

22. Change is messy in the middle and will shake up the fence-sitters. Give it time so you make it to the pay-off.

23. Selling is old-school. Today's school requires you be a student of human motivation and use discovery as your guidebook.

24. Acknowledging desired behaviors with a reward before you make it a rule will help a sales force embrace qualification adjustments.

25. The partnership between corporate and the field must be fully engaged, aware and appreciative of one another to create positive results.

26. Pink sky at night thinkers combine elevated vision and tactical sculpting.

27. The three areas for focus to get the biggest return in results are these: 1) creating an opportunity-focused culture, 2) starting new consultants strong, and 3) building pockets of passion through leadership development.

28. To build trust, you have to be trustworthy.

29. ESP will help you diagnose issues and spotlight the power of sales force count.

30. In order for leaders to grow, leaders must get wild: full of wonder, inspiring, loud in their vision and delicious in their spirits.

Sharon Morgan Tahaney